MY WEST SIDE STORY

My West Side Story

A Memoir

George Chakiris
with Lindsay Harrison

Guilford, Connecticut

An imprint of The Rowman & Littlefield Publishing Group, Inc.
4501 Forbes Boulevard, Suite 200, Lanham, Maryland 20706
www.rowman.com

Distributed by NATIONAL BOOK NETWORK

British Library Cataloguing in Publication Information Available

Library of Congress Cataloging-in-Publication Data

Names: Chakiris, George, author. | Harrison, Lindsay, author.
Title: My West Side Story : a memoir / by George Chakiris with Lindsay Harrison.
Description: Lanham, MD : Lyons Press, 2021. | Includes index. | Summary: "George Chakiris famously played the angry gang leader Bernardo in the film version of West Side Story (1961), for which he won an Oscar for best supporting actor. "—Provided by publisher.
Identifiers: LCCN 2020038087 (print) | LCCN 2020038088 (ebook) | ISBN 9781493055470 (cloth) | ISBN 9781493055487 (epub)
Subjects: LCSH: Chakiris, George. | Motion picture actors and actresses—United States—Biography. | Dancers—United States—Biography. | West Side story (Motion picture)
Classification: LCC PN2287.C465 A3 2021 (print) | LCC PN2287.C465 (ebook) | DDC 791.4308/092 [B] —dc23
LC record available at https://lccn.loc.gov/2020038087
LC ebook record available at https://lccn.loc.gov/2020038088

♾️™ The paper used in this publication meets the minimum requirements of American National Standard for Information Sciences—Permanence of Paper for Printed Library Materials, ANSI/NISO Z39.48-1992.

"No matter how dark the moment, love and hope are always possible."

—GEORGE CHAKIRIS

TABLE OF CONTENTS

INTRODUCTION

My name is George Chakiris—or, for the purpose of this book, Bernardo in the immortal film *West Side Story*.

For decades I've been urged by friends and colleagues to write a book about how my life came to intersect with what's been called "the best-loved musical of all time" and "one of the greatest entertainments in the history of motion pictures." *West Side Story* opened on Broadway on September 26, 1957, kicking off its run of 732 performances. The film premiered on October 18, 1961, and instantly became a global sensation. It won an unprecedented ten Oscars at the 1962 Academy Awards, including one for Best Motion Picture and one for me, for Best Supporting Actor.

No doubt about it, I had a lot of stories to tell, about myself and about the extraordinary experience of making this movie; but thanks to some combination of life, my tendency to be intensely private, and not being sure anyone would still care, it became one of those things that was easier to put off until "someday."

Any concerns I might have had that *West Side Story* lost its relevance over all these years have dissipated. It was honored as the Best Classic DVD at the 2011 Satellite Awards for its 50th Anniversary Edition. That same year Rita Moreno, Russ Tamblyn, and I left our footprints and signatures in the hallowed cement forecourt of Hollywood's famed Grauman's Chinese Theatre next to Natalie Wood's; and to this day I'm asked to give countless interviews and invited to appear at *West Side Story* celebrations around the world.

And then, along came the news of a major resurgence. On December 10, 2019, previews for *West Side Story* began on Broadway, leading to opening night on February 6, 2020; and none other than Steven Spielberg has filmed a remake of *West Side Story*, to be released on December 18, 2020. On one hand, I wasn't surprised that one of the most acclaimed directors in the business, who can write his own ticket in the film industry, had chosen "the best-loved musical of all time" as his next major project. On the other hand, with no disrespect intended, I started imagining audiences flocking to see *West Side Story: A Steven Spielberg Film* without knowing and fully appreciating the brilliant, complex template Spielberg had to work from.

Out of curiosity, I began looking online for a book that gave a fairly comprehensive overview of how *West Side Story* was born, how it progressed, and how close it came to never existing at all. I couldn't find one.

Finally, it felt as if there was no way around it—"someday" had arrived.

My West Side Story, then, is an overall look at how this theatrical and cinematic landmark evolved from a conversation in Jerome Robbins's Manhattan apartment between him, Arthur Laurents, and Leonard Bernstein to ten Oscars, three Golden Globes, two Tony Awards, and a Grammy.

And, because this book is called *My West Side Story*, it's also a personal memoir. While *West Side Story* obviously changed my life in more ways than I can count, it didn't begin it, and it didn't end it. From my early years as a chorus dancer in Hollywood, working with such icons as Rosemary Clooney, Gene Kelly, Gower Champion, Cyd Charisse, Debbie Reynolds, and Marilyn Monroe; to being cast in the London production of *West Side Story* and then the movie itself; to a wealth of stage, film, and television roles that landed me in the company of everyone from Yul Brynner to Judy Garland to Liza Minnelli to Marlene Dietrich to the incomparable Elaine Stritch; to an abundance of some of the most extraordinary friends anyone could ask for, I've been blessed with a life that far exceeded my childhood dreams, a life it would be ungrateful of me not to talk about.

Chapter One

An editor named Ellery Sedgwick once said, "Autobiographies ought to begin with Chapter Two." I smiled when I came across that, because I get it. We've all read memoirs in which the author goes into such exhaustive detail about their childhood that we're already tired of them by the time they reach puberty.

Every life, like every good story, has a backdrop that gives it depth and context and texture, but I promise to do my best to accomplish that without assuming you're curious about what I wore on my first day of kindergarten.

My parents, Steven and Zoe Chakiris, were extraordinary people. Somehow they managed to build a strong, loving, committed marriage and family from the world's most unromantic courtship—or, to put it more accurately, no courtship at all.

My beautiful father (center) at age fourteen

My paternal grandparents immigrated to America from a Greek village in Asia Minor with their children when my uncle Andy was fourteen and my father was twelve.

Eight years later my grandfather, finding himself with two sons of marrying age, did what any responsible, self-respecting Greek patriarch would do: He traveled back to that Greek village in Asia Minor, retrieved two attractive, appropriate young women, and presented them to Dad and Uncle Andy with an unceremonious, "This one's for you, and this one's for you."

Incredibly, that worked. For both couples. For a lifetime. No protests, no hesitation, no questions asked. The only comment I remember my mother ever making about it was, "I'm glad I got the good-looking one."

She also got the sweetest, most devoted, most responsible man I've ever known. My father was an irresistible combination of dreamer and realist, a hard-working man with a beautiful singing voice and the soul of an artist. His sister, my aunt Sophia, wrote a book about our family in which she said that Dad grew up wanting to be an actor, which always fascinated me—what on earth would have inspired a young boy in a small Greek village in Asia Minor to even think of such a thing? Then again, he obviously had an adventurous streak. He used to get on a train from time to time when he and his family were living in Florida, not to run away from home but just to explore, and I have a picture of him and a couple of his friends when he was fifteen and dressed like a cowboy. He had a great sense of humor, an infectious laugh, and the world's worst poker face. My brother Harry and I played a lot of pinochle with him, and we never had to wonder how he felt about the hand he'd been dealt.

My mother was one of those rare people who was born with a natural moral and ethical compass, and who could have fit in perfectly at a truck stop diner or Buckingham Palace. No matter where we went, everyone lit up when they saw her, as if she was the one person they were hoping to run into, because she was just so wonderful to be around. She was also a brilliant seamstress and had the patience of a saint with me and my siblings, which can't always have been easy—Mom was forty-five when she gave birth to my youngest sister Athena, who's still my closest friend and confidant, and my teenage sisters made sure she knew how mortified they were to have a pregnant mom.

These two world-class parents worked hard to support their family, and they raised seven children who never doubted for a moment that we were loved, we were safe, and we were cared for. We were very blessed.

For the first three years of my life, we lived upstairs from my grandfather's confectionery and beer garden in Norwood, Ohio. I remember a patio with cherry trees and wrought iron tables and chairs . . . icy, snowy, bitterly cold winters ... the Ohio River overflowing its banks ... and literally being a kid in a candy store, stealing as much as I wanted whenever I wanted and never being scolded for it.

My parents worked at the confectionery and returned their weekly paycheck to my grandfather, who then gave my parents enough money to maybe see a movie. This "old world" arrangement probably sounded reasonable when they all agreed to it, and my father, of course, had to respect his father. But my mother always knew it was wrong.

Finally, when I was three, Dad decided that everyone would be happier and healthier if he packed up his wife and children and moved us to the warm sun and independence of the South. We spent some time living in Arizona, and in Florida. Then, when I was six, we settled in Arizona again—Mom, Dad, five kids, and all our belongings crowded into the family car, en route to a modest house outside of Tucson. Mom and Dad found work at a laundry, Mom as a seamstress and Dad driving a laundry truck, and I started school.

Isn't it interesting how we tend to look back on most of our childhood years through kind of a filmy haze, but a few random details are preserved in our minds with such crystal clarity that it's almost as if they just happened?

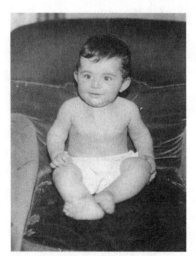

Eight months old in 1932

Three years old in 1935

I remember sharing sleeping space with my older sister Catherine.

I remember long walks in the cold Arizona winters to retrieve kerosene for the heater in our house.

I remember how much Catherine and I loved to dance, almost from the moment we were born, and how we'd dance in our living room at night and watch our reflection in the windows.

I remember selling newspapers with my brother Harry on a street corner in downtown Tucson. He's eighteen months older than I am, and he's such a good big brother that on the rare occasions when we got into a tussle, he'd always let me win.

I remember a Sunday when I was nine years old. December 7, 1941— "a date that will live in infamy." The Japanese had bombed Pearl Harbor, and the grownups were very upset about it. I didn't understand exactly what was going on, I just knew that something terrible and scary had happened to our country. We loved our country. We were proud of our country. We were Americans, and we felt good about being Americans in

Me with my brother Harry, 1939

the world. But we had an enemy. Not a Republican or a Democrat, not across the aisle, but far away, across oceans, something called the Axis Powers, a team of Germany, Italy, and Japan who wanted to dominate us. We knew we would be all right, though, because we had a great man to lead us through the war, a man named President Roosevelt, fearless and respected and much loved. I remember my mom crying the day we lost him.

But mostly, I remember the movies.

From the time I was a little boy, movies enthralled me. They weren't an escape. I had a nice life. I wasn't looking for an escape. Instead, movies were a destination, a beautiful Technicolor fantasy world I could live in for a couple of hours, a world full of gorgeous people and places and stories and, always, music. I wasn't interested in movies with soldiers and guns and blood and violence, just beauty and grace and happy endings and music that would stay with me long after I left the theater.

Back row: me; my sisters Catherine, Virginia, and Viola; and my brother Harry
Front row: our mother, my brother Steve, and our father, 1939

I went to the movies every single Saturday. And I admit it, there were many days when I turned away from my walk to school and headed downtown instead to immerse myself in a dark theater that was always so much more mesmerizing than a classroom. I was good at remembering songs from the musicals, and I'd sing them to myself on the way home, convinced that my soprano voice sounded every bit as good as Helen Forrest, a singer I loved listening to on the radio. My family and friends were great, but nothing could compare to being by myself, reliving every glorious stolen moment in some magical location where I could spend time with beautiful people like Betty Grable and Tyrone Power and Carmen Miranda. In fact, it was on that historic Sunday, Pearl Harbor Day, that I was walking up the street in a hurry to get to the theater when a couple of kids pulled up in a big truck full of "EXTRA" newspapers and asked if I wanted to make some money helping them sell them. Not a chance. I was on my way to see a Carmen Miranda musical.

I started dreaming about living in that movie world. Being rich and famous wasn't even a tiny fraction of the equation. The dream was about being part of that transformative magic that, no matter what else was going on in my life, always managed to fully engross me. It was about doing for other people what movies did for me, entertaining them, sending them away with a brand new song to sing to themselves and the feeling that they'd been transported to a whole different place for a little while that they could look back on and revisit whenever they wanted.

I just had no idea how to get to that world from our modest little house in Arizona.

When I was about ten years old, I was introduced to a man named Eduardo Caso. He was a former British radio performer who'd come from England to a Tucson sanatorium to recover from tuberculosis. He was so grateful for the restorative sunshine and the people that he decided to stay and "give back" to the city through his gifts as a teacher and singer. He ended up "giving back" by founding and being the choirmaster of the Tucson Arizona Boys Chorus. Shy as I was, I still had my Helen Forrest soprano voice, so I tried out and was lucky enough to be accepted. Suddenly, there I was onstage with two dozen other "ambassadors in Levis," as the chorus came to be known, singing for this amazing, supportive, talented man I couldn't have admired more.

We started to become a bit famous in Arizona and the Southwest, which led to one of the most unforgettable experiences of my childhood—the Tucson Arizona Boys Chorus was invited to sing for the Easter sunrise service at the Grand Canyon at 5:00 a.m., before the world was awake. I don't have words for how humbling and uplifting it was for this introverted little boy to be part of something so breathtaking, so almost magical. . . .

And then when I was twelve, just as my budding singing career was about to blossom, my dad announced that we were moving to Long Beach, in Southern California, where he'd always wanted us to live. The last thing I wanted to do was leave the Boys Chorus. The end of a dream. O, the tragedy.

But Mr. Caso, my hero, saved the day and encouraged me to audition for a very famous Long Beach choir called the St. Luke's Choristers. He felt very confident that I'd be accepted, and he promised I would love it. So once the family was settled into our new home, I headed straight to St. Luke's Episcopal Church and auditioned for the Choristers' founder and choirmaster, a well-known music conductor named William Ripley Dorr. Mr. Caso was right. I was accepted, and I loved it.

We rehearsed every Thursday evening and sang at St. Luke's Episcopal Church every Sunday. The other boys were great. In fact, when I mentioned that our neighbors were letting me use their piano, one of them even taught me to play the first movement of Beethoven's Moonlight Sonata. I was so excited, and it felt like such an accomplishment.

But don't get me wrong. I'd heard when I joined the Choristers that they'd also performed in many movies! I admit it, from the very beginning, I was a little jealous and a little restless, wondering if and when that might happen again.

I didn't have to wonder for long.

Shortly after I joined the choir, the St. Luke's Choristers were hired to sing for, and appear in, a concert sequence in a movie called *Song of Love*, about musicians Clara and Robert Schumann, starring Katharine Hepburn, Paul Henreid, and Robert Walker.

St. Luke's Choristers, Long Beach, 1947. I'm in the second row, first on the left.

I couldn't believe it. *The* Katharine Hepburn, Paul Henreid, and Robert Walker?! Whom I'd seen and admired in about a thousand movies?! And if that weren't enough to take my breath away, we'd be reporting for work at—unbelievably—MGM Studios! My personal Promised Land, the birthplace of my childhood dreams! My feet didn't touch the ground for weeks.

MGM did not disappoint.

Just being waved through the guarded gates at the entrance with the rest of the choristers made me feel privileged, like an insider.

Then there was the lot itself, a massive collage of worlds with surprises around every corner—a Western town here, a real live pirate ship on a lake there, New York brownstones, and a cozy suburban neighborhood overlooking a horse pasture. . . .

The streets were filled with crews bustling around in all directions, transporting giant lighting and sound equipment and racks of every imaginable wardrobe item. On one of our first days at the studio we were headed for our soundstage when, in the midst of all that busy-ness, Frank Sinatra strolled by on his way to work as if he were a normal person.

It was thrilling and surreal.

As underage kids, we choristers were required to attend three hours of school on the lot every day for the two weeks we were there. We were supposed to care about math and geography. Why? Here? When God knows who might be passing by right outside the door at any given moment? Seriously?

The only memorable thing about the MGM school was this impossibly gorgeous girl I saw there a few times. None of us could take our eyes off of her. From what I was told, she was fifteen years old, and she'd just finished making a movie called *Cynthia*, in which she'd received her first screen kiss.

I stood next to her when we were all invited to watch an up-and-coming tenor named Mario Lanza record a song for his latest film, but I couldn't work up the courage to say hello to her. And then there was the Halloween party at the MGM schoolhouse for all the kids on the lot. One

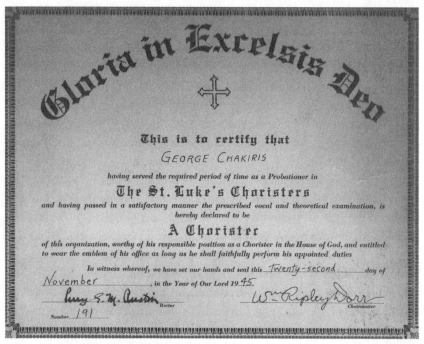

Gloria in Excelsis Deo

✠

This is to certify that

GEORGE CHAKIRIS

having served the required period of time as a Probationer in

The St. Luke's Choristers

and having passed in a satisfactory manner the prescribed vocal and theoretical examination, is hereby declared to be

A Chorister

of this organization, worthy of his responsible position as a Chorister in the House of God, and entitled to wear the emblem of his office as long as he shall faithfully perform his appointed duties

In witness whereof, we have set our hands and seal this Twenty-second *day of* November, *in the Year of Our Lord 19*45.

Rector   Choirmaster

Number 191

My St. Luke's Choristers Certificate

of my fellow choristers actually had the nerve to ask her to dance, and she politely said yes. I stood on the sidelines, admiring her and envying him.

My one chance to ask Elizabeth Taylor to dance, and I was too shy to even imagine it.

We filmed our scenes for *Song of Love* on a cavernous soundstage. Every time someone walked through that stage door, I thought I was going to be discovered. I was twelve, and you hear stories, right?

It didn't happen. I left the studio undiscovered. But what did happen, thanks to those amazing two weeks, was confirmation that being part of that magical world was exactly what I wanted and exactly where I wanted to be. It wasn't an idle, far-away dream anymore; it was a wide-awake certainty. I still just had no idea how to go about it.

Like my older siblings, after graduating from Jefferson Junior High, I went to Woodrow Wilson High School in Long Beach. I was more resolute than ever about skipping school and going to see a movie, *any* movie, but most definitely any movie starring Fred Astaire and Ginger Rogers. Those two stars dancing together were perfect, like one, like silk, weightless, defying gravity, art in motion. When I found out their movie *The Barclays of Broadway* was coming, I looked forward to it like people look forward to the Super Bowl. I had to see it, and I had to see the first showing on the first night or die trying. It turned out to be a good thing I did—I got sick on the bus on the way home from the theater with what turned out to be the mumps. If I hadn't seen it exactly when I did, I would have missed it completely, and it would have felt like a devastating loss.

I can't begin to count the number of times I took the bus to downtown Long Beach to see the latest movie musical; but my favorite thing to do when the movies were over was to walk home alone on the beach and relive them, absorb them, almost wrap myself up in them and be part of them for as long as I could before ordinary life intruded again.

So looking back, I guess it was almost inevitable that one of the first schoolmates I noticed at Woodrow Wilson High was a girl named Joan Scanlon. She was exotic, and romantic, and most of all, she happened to be a really gifted dancer. She and her dance partner performed at various high school functions and assemblies, which made her kind of a celebrity

After school, Long Beach, 1948

Fifteen years old in Long Beach, 1947

In Long Beach with my
eight-month-old sister
Athena, 1947

Portrait at fifteen years old, 1947

With my beautiful mother

in my eyes; it turned out she'd actually studied dance at the highly respected Audrey Share School in Long Beach.

Scholastic Art Award Certificate of Merit, 1949

To my amazement, she'd noticed me too. And when her dance partner left to join the Coast Guard, Joan completely shocked me by asking me to take his place. I couldn't believe it, but I wasn't about to say no, if only to spend time with her. Audrey Share helped create some routines, Joan and I worked hard and practiced tirelessly, and finally we made our debut together at a high school assembly. I was terrified, but in spite of that, it went perfectly. It was a huge surprise to discover that, while I'd always hated being the center of attention (and still do), I loved dancing for an audience. I loved the feeling that, for a few short minutes, I might have been part of a little magic myself. It gave me the most extraordinary sense of accomplishment, of being completely happy, of just being complete.

I was joyfully hooked.

When I graduated from Woodrow Wilson High, I followed Joan to Long Beach City College and worked on weekends in the meat market of a grocery store to help support myself. Joan and I took an acting class and spent a lot of time together in general, and she started talking pretty dreamily about a place called the American School of Dance in Hollywood. Apparently Leslie Caron studied there. Cyd Charisse studied there. That was all I needed to hear.

I hopped on the train from Long Beach to Hollywood one morning to watch a class. No celebrities were in the class that day, but it didn't matter. Here were all these people, learning and doing what I'd been wanting to learn and do for as long as I could remember. I wanted in. No matter what it took, I wanted to study at the American School of Dance. With my family cheering me on, I packed a bag, said goodbye to Long Beach, and headed for Hollywood.

I also essentially said goodbye to a future with Joan. Over the course of our few years together, even though nothing had ever happened between us, I'd started having romantic feelings for her. In fact, I thought I wanted to marry her. Unfortunately there was a guy named Dino who seemed to like both Joan and me and started hanging out with us. I thought he was odd and kind of kept my distance from him. But Joan liked him, and I began to notice that when the three of us were together, I always felt like an outsider. So I left it at a friendship with Joan and let it go at that. I have no idea whatever happened to Dino, but Joan will always have a special place in my heart. To this day I model my handwriting after hers and think of her every time I sign my name.

I was nineteen years old when I started studying at the American School of Dance at 7021 Hollywood Boulevard. It was my first formal training in anything related to the performing arts.

I rented a room in a boardinghouse a few blocks from the school, and to support myself I found a job as an office boy in the advertising department of the May Company in downtown Los Angeles. I took the now-defunct train to the May Company and back, worked from 8:00 a.m. until 5:00 p.m. five days a week, and then took two dance classes every night and one on Saturdays.

I was so happy. I woke up every morning looking forward to the day and night ahead, and I quickly became friends with a lot of my classmates. Several of them were working as chorus dancers in the movie *Singin' in the Rain*, and it was worth the sleep deprivation to go out for a bite to eat after our second class to hear their fabulous stories about Debbie Reynolds, Gene Kelly, Donald O'Connor, Cyd Charisse, and a gifted young newcomer named Rita Moreno. I soaked up those stories and hoped I'd have some of my own to tell someday. Those were wonderful times. I still cherish them.

Mack Sennett lived at the top of 7021 Hollywood Boulevard. After reading his subscription copies of the *Hollywood Reporter* and *Variety*, he would leave them at the school's reception desk for everyone else to enjoy. It never occurred to me to even glance at them. If only I had,

In class at the American School of Dance,
about 1951

and then saved them. Hollywood history at my fingertips, and I paid no attention because, I'm embarrassed to admit, I had no idea who Mack Sennett was. Believe me, I've since found out. Actor. Director. Producer. Founder of his own movie studio. Known in the film industry as the King of Comedy. And I'd never heard of him. I definitely needed to start paying more attention.

It was an unbelievable shot in the arm when, after about six months of studying at the American School of Dance, I was given a scholarship. I no longer had to pay for classes! And all I had to do in exchange was clean the studios at the end of the day—the walls of mirrors, the floors and the reception area, the dressing rooms—and lock up. My pleasure!

Once those nightly duties were taken care of and I'd double-checked the school doors to make sure they were locked safe and sound, I'd walk up Hollywood Boulevard to my room at the boardinghouse, which took me right past Grauman's Chinese Theatre. It was quiet in those days at that hour, not a tourist in sight, and I'd always stop, an audience of one looking at the movie stars' footprints in the theater's legendary forecourt. I had all those iconic footprints to myself, night after night for as long as

Head shot, 1950

I wanted, my own sweet, peaceful time to hope and dream. I never dared to include the dream that someday my footprints might be there too.

Even when you're only nineteen years old, a schedule of almost fifty hours commuting and working downtown, eleven dance classes per week, and a custodial job at the school can wear you out. I was beginning to wonder how long I could keep this up when the school's founder Eugene Loring, a very important choreographer in the ballet and movie worlds, approached several of us one night after class.

It seems Mr. Loring, who ran the American School of Dance, was choreographing a film for producer/director Stanley Kramer, and he needed sixty union male dancers for a dream sequence in the movie. There weren't that many male dancers in the Screen Extras Guild at the time, so a few of us non-union dancers got to audition. And I got the job. I was about to dance in my first film. A Stanley Kramer film. Stanley Kramer, who would go on to produce such classics as *Inherit the Wind*, *Judgment at Nuremberg*, and *Guess Who's Coming to Dinner*.

This particular movie, though, was called *The 5,000 Fingers of Dr. T*, and on paper, my role didn't exactly have the words "fast track to stardom" written all over it. My fifty-nine fellow chorus dancers and I appeared in a scene in which the young lead, Tommy Rettig, had a nightmare that involved all kinds of musical instruments.

I was a trombone. But wait, there's more—to make us instruments look really nightmarish and otherworldly, we were spray-painted green every morning before we got into our costumes. I managed to embarrass myself by breaking a real trombone during one of the takes, but other than that, the shoot went smoothly.

I wasn't all that surprised this time that no one burst through the stage door and discovered me while we were filming. But in a way, playing a dancing green trombone in *The 5,000 Fingers of Dr. T* was my first big break.

Thanks to my paycheck for that job, I didn't have to work downtown at the May Company anymore to pay my bills.

I was able to move out of my room in the boardinghouse and into a studio apartment on Pinehurst Road in the lower Hollywood Hills.

I got to focus 100 percent of my energy on the career I'd dreamed of since I was a little boy in Tucson, skipping school to board a bus and go to the movies.

And I could afford to join the union, which allowed me to start going out on real auditions, which ultimately led me so much farther than all those childhood dreams had ever taken me.

Chapter Two

THE CHARACTER OF MAGGIE IN TENNESSEE WILLIAMS'S *CAT ON A HOT TIN ROOF* has a line that goes, "You can be young without money, but you can't be old without it." The older I get and the more I look back, the more I appreciate how true that is.

The apartment I moved into when I left my room at the boarding-house was small and very modest. It was on the second floor of a four-unit building, with a street address that added up to seven, my favorite number. The kitchenette had a hot plate and an ice box, and an iceman brought a fresh block of ice every two weeks. That was all I needed. I could easily walk to Hollywood Boulevard in one direction and the Hollywood Bowl in the other; but I felt like I was living in a hideaway, a private little knotty pine cabin in the woods, away from everyone and everything. I filled the air around me with Judy Garland's *Miss Show Business* album, and Respighi's *The Pines of Rome* and *The Fountains of Rome*. I had everything I could have asked for and more, and I still ache just a little when I hear that music and get transported back to those sweet, simple nights.

Many of my classmates at the American School of Dance were as broke as I was. Three of us—Lisa Lang, Michael Stevens, and I—would pool our money to buy a loaf of bread, a can of tuna, and a small jar of mayonnaise and call it dinner. I remember making and loving ketchup sandwiches.

It was all good. Life was full of hope and possibilities and friends who cheered each other on. We were happy, living day to day, moment to moment, audition to audition, and happiness is its own kind of nourishment.

There was no such thing as an audition or a job that didn't matter. I never once included the word *only* when I referred to myself as a chorus dancer. I was proud and grateful to be one, and as I learned from my brief stint as a dancing green trombone, you never knew who might be watching and what other projects and connections any job might lead to.

You also never knew when you might find yourself working next to a star you'd admired for as long as you could remember.

I was hired for the chorus of *The Farmer Takes a Wife*. I was in such awe that on one of my shooting days I had to excuse myself to go to the men's room to throw up. No, it wasn't the brilliance of the material that overwhelmed me. It was finding myself on the same soundstage as 20th Century Fox's biggest star and moneymaker, Betty Grable.

Betty Grable wasn't a superstar for no reason. She sang. She was a smart, talented actress with a delightful sense of humor. And she was a wonderful dancer. She'd started her film career when she was twelve years old, so she "got" performing. She understood it. She also had amazing intuitive instincts, which led to impeccable judgment as an actress, singer, and dancer. There was disarming subtlety in her work—she never hit her audience over the head with anything; and I was pleasantly surprised to

My personally signed photo of Rosalind Russell from *The Girl Rush*, 1953

Partnering Rosalind Russell in *The Girl Rush*, 1954

discover that beyond being a beautiful performer, she was great fun to be around. Everyone who worked with her loved Betty Grable.

Her choreographer on *The Farmer Takes a Wife* was also one of the best, a man named Jack Cole. He was a legend at creating signature musical numbers for female stars, like Rita Hayworth's iconic scenes in *Gilda*, and it was a joy to watch the process of him doing exactly the same thing for Betty Grable. Unfortunately, studios who put stars under contract didn't always provide them with their best vehicles, so it was no surprise to anyone, including Betty, that *The Farmer Takes a Wife* didn't make it onto her Greatest Hits list. But Jack Cole also choreographed for her a year or two later in a film that was worthy of her, *Meet Me After the Show*. She was spectacular in that movie, which had a really good script and sensational musical numbers. (In fact, if you look closely, you'll see a young Gwen Verdon dancing right next to her.)

I remember thinking as I left the soundstage on my last day of *The Farmer Takes a Wife* that whatever my next chorus job was, it was bound to be a big disappointment after working with *the* Betty Grable, the highest paid woman in the country at the time.

I was wrong.

Betty Grable was in the middle of a contract dispute with 20th Century Fox at the time, during which they replaced her on her next scheduled film with another exquisite, incredibly charismatic actress.

The movie was *Gentlemen Prefer Blondes*, which Fox had purchased as a vehicle for Betty Grable. Her replacement was a knockout in her late twenties named Marilyn Monroe. I was hired to be a chorus dancer in a number called "Diamonds Are a Girl's Best Friend."

Marilyn had a quality that can't be taught, or created with wardrobe and makeup, a quality you're either born with or you're not—when she was on camera, no matter who else was on camera with her, you couldn't not look at her.

She didn't engage in small talk, not because she was unfriendly but because she was just very focused on her work. Between takes while she filmed her scenes with us chorus dancers, she didn't disappear into her dressing room or demand attention from hair and makeup. She simply went back to her starting position and waited for her cue.

I happened to witness a moment during a break while filming "Diamonds" that made a lasting impression on me. Jack Cole was Marilyn's choreographer, of course, and he was standing close to her, directly in front of her, presumably giving her notes about the number, although I couldn't hear what he was saying. She was nodding a little, seeming to be listening intently and very politely. Unbeknownst to Jack, Marilyn's acting coach and constant companion Natasha Lytess was standing right behind him, silently shaking her head "no!", as in, I thought, "Pay no attention to him, we'll discuss this later." Marilyn could obviously see her peripherally, but she never broke eye contact with Jack or showed any sign at all that she was seemingly being hit with two completely conflicting messages at the same time. During the brief exchange she managed to be respectful to

Marilyn Monroe in the "Diamonds are a Girl's Best Friend" number from *Gentlemen Prefer Blondes*, 1953. I am directly to the right.

both relationships, and it was almost mesmerizing to see how gracefully and sweetly she pulled it off.

One day after rehearsals there was a party on the soundstage for the cast and crew. When Marilyn made her typical quiet entrance, my friend and fellow dancer Drusilla Davis turned to me and said, "Why don't I ask her to give you a kiss on the cheek?"

I was horrified. "No!" I loudly whispered to her. "Absolutely not! Don't you dare!"

Drusilla, always entertained by my shyness, did it anyway. Marilyn looked over at me, then turned back to Drusilla and said, "But I don't know him."

That still touches me to this day. Somewhere in there was a woman who was as shy as I was, at least back then in the early 1950s, maybe before she became overwhelmed by all the expectations involved in being Marilyn Monroe.

I got to work with her again, first as an extra in *How to Marry a Millionaire,* and then more memorably on a movie called *There's No Business Like Show Business.* Marilyn was surrounded by an incredible cast in *There's No Business Like Show Business* that included Ethel Merman, Donald O'Connor, Dan Dailey, Mitzi Gaynor, and Johnnie Ray; and the film was being choreographed by one of the best, most delightful choreographers of his era, Robert Alton.

There was a number in the film called "Lazy," with Marilyn, Donald, and Mitzi. Donald and Mitzi were right on time the morning they were to start shooting it and waited impatiently for Marilyn, who finally showed up at 3:00 p.m. Easy for me to say, since I wasn't in the scene, but I remember thinking, "Hey, at least she's worth waiting for."

Even though Robert Alton was choreographing *There's No Business Like Show Business,* Marilyn insisted that no one but Jack Cole choreograph the "Heat Wave" number in the film. Marilyn understandably trusted him and was comfortable with him. But still, it was awkward, especially for Bob Alton, to bring in a separate choreographer for just that one number, and Bob was under no obligation to agree to it.

Rather than simply refuse, or argue with her, he chose to inspire her to change her mind instead.

Working as an extra behind Marilyn Monroe in *How to Marry a Millionaire*, 1953

First, he took the time to set up a screening of "I'm Going to File My Claim," a song Marilyn does in the film *River of No Return*, choreographed by Jack Cole. Another male dancer, Pepe De Chazza, and I were allowed to go to the screening. The song itself is filled with double entendres, which Pepe and I both found really funny but Bob found vulgar. It probably was. Marilyn performed it on a platform for an audience of guys. In one segment the camera is behind the men's heads and slightly below her waist level, and one of her asides to the guys is, "Mmmmm. Lookin' for nuggets?" It was funny, and it was Jack. It was also "mission accomplished"—Bob now had an idea of Jack's style as interpreted by Marilyn so that he could tailor his choreography to what she seemed to appreciate.

He then spent four weeks putting the "Heat Wave" number together his way, with his assistant choreographer Joan Bayley standing in for Marilyn and four of us male dancers behind her. When he finally felt it was ready to show to Marilyn, he summoned her to one of the massive rehearsal halls on the 20th Century Fox lot.

It was a typical brilliantly sunny summer day in Hollywood. Marilyn came walking in by herself. She was wearing a soft orange knit dress, and with the sun behind her we got an opaque view of her hypnotic silhouette as she walked from the huge open doors to the group that was gathered to perform for her. After the usual greetings, she took her seat and watched Joan Bayley and us chorus dancers perform "Heat Wave" as choreographed for her by Robert Alton. When it was finished, Marilyn very politely thanked Bob and everyone else and left.

Jack Cole ended up choreographing the famous, or infamous, "Heat Wave" number in *There's No Business Like Show Business*, and Bob Alton graciously stepped aside and let it happen. Despite Ed Sullivan calling it "one of the most flagrant violations of good taste" he'd ever seen, I happened to think it was great. As I'd personally witnessed with Betty Grable, and with Marilyn on "Diamonds Are a Girl's Best Friend," Jack more than lived up to his reputation as a brilliant choreographer on "Heat Wave."

Again, in spite of Ed Sullivan's disapproval, it was signature Jack Cole. He was also known for occasionally enhancing the dance numbers he created for the women he showcased with bits of humor in the moves themselves and in the asides he came up with that weren't in the written lyrics. A classic example is Jane Russell's "Ain't There Anyone Here for Love?" segment in *Gentlemen Prefer Blondes*. Jane's singing, surrounded by a bunch of exercising male athletes. At one point, thanks entirely to Jack, she picks up a couple of tennis rackets and says, "Doubles, anyone?", followed by, "Doesn't anyone wanna play?" Incidentally, a bit of trivia: That number ends with Jane being knocked into the pool by one of the athletes. It was an accident, unscripted, but they kept it in anyway, right on through the guys pulling a very gorgeous, very wet Jane Russell out of the pool.

At any rate, next time you watch Marilyn Monroe's torrid performance of "Heat Wave" in *There's No Business Like Show Business*, notice her occasional asides when she's referring to the different temperatures in the newspaper and remember to thank Jack Cole . . . and Marilyn, for her refusal to let anyone else but him create that number for her. Predictably, there were those who thought her insistence on switching choreographers for that one song was just another example of Marilyn Monroe being difficult and demanding. Personally, I thought it was brave of her to pay attention to her instincts and speak up for what she knew was right for her.

Many decades later I accepted an invitation to participate in a documentary about her. I said then what I'll always say—I'm sorry I didn't get to know her, but I'll always be so grateful that I had the pleasure of working with her, not once but twice. One of my favorite credits is being able to say I was one of the guys behind Marilyn Monroe in the "Diamonds Are a Girl's Best Friend" number. She more than earned her iconic place in show business history; her death, however it happened, was tragic and came too soon. It couldn't have been easy being Marilyn Monroe.

Then there was *Give a Girl a Break*, the "Applause" number, with Debbie Reynolds and Gower Champion. What's not to appreciate? Debbie was all of twenty years old, so strong and so confident. If she wasn't comfortable with the way a take was going, she'd suddenly stop dancing. Just stop. A voice would come booming through the soundstage speakers: "Debbie, don't stop unless we stop you." She kept on doing it. She knew when the number was going exactly right and when it wasn't, and she trusted her instincts more than she trusted "the Suits."

Soon after I worked with Gene Kelly in *Brigadoon*, my first movie with him but not my last. The Scottish Sword Dance. Cut from the finished film, but still, Gene Kelly! And a valuable learning experience—in case you've been wondering, if you ever have your heart set on getting shin splints, all you have to do is dance on the balls of your feet for days on end.

And by the time *There's No Business Like Show Business* came along, I'd already done a film with Robert Alton: *White Christmas* with Bing Crosby, Rosemary Clooney, Danny Kaye, and Vera-Ellen. I knew going in what a gifted, generous, friendly, funny man Alton was and what a joy it was to work for him. All the dancers loved working for Bob. He was good

Working in the chorus of *Brigadoon* at MGM, 1952. I am at far left.

to everyone and knew everybody by name, and he helped set the tone for one of the happiest, most pleasant movies I've ever been part of.

White Christmas was a fantastic experience in so many ways. And by the way, before I forget, I do want to correct what's apparently become a common misconception about that movie. I can't count the number of times I've heard it stated as a fact that Bob Fosse was an uncredited choreographer on *White Christmas*. Believe me, I'm a Bob Fosse fan, but that "fact" is completely untrue. Take it from me, or from anyone else who worked on that film and was on the set from beginning to end—Robert Alton choreographed it. Fosse had nothing to do with it, was never there, not once, nor was his name ever mentioned.

From our first day on the set of *White Christmas*, Rosemary Clooney immediately insisted that we all call her Rosie. She was so accessible, a warm, darling woman, madly in love with her new husband José Ferrer, whom she talked to at least fifty times a day (okay, maybe ten) on the very non-private soundstage wall phone. As if I didn't already think Rosie was amazing enough, she also turned out to be a close friend of screen goddess

Marlene Dietrich. Dietrich came to the set one day to visit her—impeccably dressed, breathtaking, looking like . . . well, looking like Marlene Dietrich. It never occurred to any of us to speak to her and maybe say hello. We couldn't possibly approach Marlene Dietrich!

Not long after we started shooting *White Christmas*, word spread throughout the male chorus dancers that four of us were going to be chosen for a featured number with Rosie, "Love You Didn't Do Right By Me." I hoped that I could be one of those four guys.

Then, during a break in filming, a dancer named Matt Mattox called and asked me to audition to be one of the dancers in an upcoming movie called *Seven Brides for Seven Brothers*. Matt was a great dancer and a terrific guy, and the movie was being choreographed by Michael Kidd, one of the best in the business. Matt was already playing one of the brothers and was sure I would love working for Michael Kidd, and he'd already recommended me.

I was flattered. I was also not interested, only because saying yes to *Seven Brides for Seven Brothers* would have meant missing out on the possibility of being in "Love You Didn't Do Right By Me" with Rosie. Every instinct in me told me I'd kick myself later if I passed up that opportunity. I made up an excuse to Matt, thanked him for thinking of me, and hung up the phone.

Call number two from Matt. *Please* come audition for this movie. I felt badly about it, but in the end, another excuse, another "thanks so much anyway."

Finally, on call number three, I couldn't bring myself to come up with yet another excuse, and the last thing I wanted to do was offend Matt. I had such respect for him. So I reluctantly said yes and told him to go ahead and set it up. Then, really not wanting to be there, I auditioned for Michael Kidd, gave one of the worst auditions of my life, and saw to it that I'd be available for that number with Rosie if they chose me.

They did choose me. I was one of the four guys dancing behind Rosemary Clooney for "Love You Didn't Do Right By Me." It was great fun. In the course of the number each of us got a medium shot with her, which ended up proving that blowing the *Seven Brides for Seven Brothers* audition was exactly the right thing to do.

My personally autoraphed photo of Rosemary Clooney
in *White Christmas*, 1954

With Rosemary Clooney in *White Christmas*, 1954

After *White Christmas* came chorus work on a Rosalind Russell movie, *The Girl Rush*, also being choreographed by Robert Alton. Robert Emmett Dolan was the producer on both films. One day during rehearsals for *The Girl Rush* he came to me with a stack of fan letters asking who the guy was with Rosemary Clooney in that number in *White Christmas*. It seems *Life* magazine had done a pictorial spread on the movie, including those shots of Rosie with us four dancers. The fans who'd written letters had enclosed the photos and drawn arrows and circles to specify that I was the guy they were asking about.

Apparently, fan mail was the 1955 version of Facebook likes and Twitter followers, because Robert Emmett Dolan was so impressed by the volume of those letters that he set up a screen test for me at Paramount.

I was thrilled, not only by the offer of a screen test but also by the generous support I found myself surrounded by for it. Mr. Dolan asked Bob Alton to direct the musical part of the test. Robert Alton, directing a screen test? How lucky was I? I even overheard Bob telling the

Hillbilly number with Rosalind Russell from *The Girl Rush*, 1954. I am at far right.

Champagne number with Gloria De Haven in *The Girl Rush*, 1954. I am at far left.

cinematographer before we started, "I want you to photograph this boy like Dietrich." I also learned that Danny Kaye, who'd been wonderful to me when we shot *White Christmas*, was instrumental in getting me tested. It's amazing how much extra confidence it gives you when you know that people you admire have your back.

I never saw the screen test; but I do remember a black-and-white scene in which a Paramount contract player named Brett Halsey and I played two sailors, and a singing and dancing test in color in which I sang, "My Romance."

Apparently it went well. Next thing I knew I was signing a seven-year contract at Paramount. Unbelievable. To congratulate me, Danny Kaye gave me a beautiful pair of gold cufflinks. I still have them, and I treasure them.

Now if I could just find a copy of that screen test, although it probably doesn't exist anymore. I would love an opportunity to see that young, hopeful boy on film today and look back at where it all started.

Warming up at home, 1955

Paramount studio photo, 1955

A contract at Paramount Pictures was more than enough to make me feel as if I'd "made it." But then, out of nowhere, came a call from Jerry Wald. Like everyone else, I was well aware of Jerry Wald, a very important producer who'd worked with everyone from Humphrey Bogart to Errol Flynn to Lauren Bacall to Kirk Douglas. My *White Christmas* scene with Rosie had caught his attention, and he wanted to meet me in his office at Columbia! I didn't happen to have a car, but my friend Drusilla Davis did, and she was kind enough to let me borrow it to go to that meeting.

Jerry Wald was warm and welcoming, and he introduced me to Columbia's drama coach, Benno Schneider, with the added comment that in his opinion, I was "the next Montgomery Clift." I was still reeling a little from that when Mr. Wald told me he was interested in arranging to have Paramount loan me out for a role in his upcoming movie for 20th Century Fox, *Peyton Place*.

Just when I thought that day couldn't get any better, I thanked Jerry Wald and Benno Schneider and said goodbye, left the building, headed for "my" (Drusilla's) car and ran into Kim Novak, who was in search of a lift to Hollywood and Vine. Right on my way home, and even if it hadn't been, I would have pretended it was. So after my meeting with Jerry Wald, who thought I was the next Montgomery Clift and wanted to talk to me about his next movie, I dropped Kim Novak off at Hollywood and Vine, drove back to my sweet little apartment, and probably didn't get a wink of sleep that night as I relived that very heady day.

I did not get the part in *Peyton Place*, but I've always wished I'd had a chance to work with Jerry Wald. He was held in such high regard in the film industry, and he obviously had a rich imagination to see me in a brief dance number with Rosemary Clooney and make the jump to picturing my potential as a dramatic actor. I was, and have always been very flattered.

By the way, I never knew what part I (badly) auditioned for in *Seven Brides for Seven Brothers*, but I know an incredibly gifted young actor and dancer named Russ Tamblyn played one of the brothers in that movie. And that role in *Peyton Place* Jerry Wald mentioned to me went to Russ Tamblyn and earned him an Academy Award nomination.

Now if I could just stop forgetting to tell Russ that story....

Shortly after I signed my Paramount contract, the studio threw a formal dinner on one of the soundstages for its contract players. I'd already met one in particular, a gorgeous nineteen-year-old Swiss actress named Ursula Andress. She was such a breath of fresh air—a great sense of humor; and in refreshing contrast to so many up-and-coming actors in town, she never seemed to take herself or the whole Hollywood thing too seriously. I sat across from her and her boyfriend that night. His name was James Dean. He seemed sweet, somewhat shy and quietly intense, and Ursula was clearly infatuated with him. The car accident that ended his life happened less than a year later.

Being free to wander around the Paramount lot was like being turned loose at Disneyland for me. I strolled onto a soundstage one day and stood about twelve feet away from this electrifying performer named Elvis Presley while he sang "Blue Suede Shoes" for a screen test for Hal Wallis. I was standing alone and it almost felt like he was performing just for me. It's fascinating how obvious it is when you find yourself watching a future superstar.

I also snuck onto another soundstage when I heard that Audrey Hepburn was shooting *Funny Face* there. They were at one end of the huge soundstage, I was at the other, being as quiet and unobtrusive as possible and hiding as best I could. But suddenly I was tapped on the shoulder and asked to leave. It turned out to be a carefully protected edict of Audrey Hepburn's that no one be allowed to watch her film, and as tempting as it was to keep trying, I never let it happen again.

I *did* get to watch Fred Astaire and Kay Thompson shoot the "Clap Yo' Hands" number for *Funny Face*, though, which more than made up for being kicked out of Audrey Hepburn's soundstage. My friend Lisa Lang and I had met Kay Thompson at Bob Alton's house once, and she was nice enough to remember us, engage in a little small talk, and let us stay for the filming. Watching her and Fred Astaire work was nothing short of amazing! She was such an extraordinary performer who had worked with Astaire, Garland, and many more when she worked at MGM. She even ventured into live performing with Kay Thompson and the Williams Brothers, one of those brothers being Andy. And in my opinion, by the way, she practically steals *Funny Face*.

But there was also business to attend to at Paramount, of course, and one of their first issues when I signed my contract was their insistence that I change my name. Their reasoning was that "Chakiris" didn't sound "commercial." But I believed then, as I believe now, that it was really because ethnic names weren't very popular in the industry in those days. They came up with "Kerris." "George Kerris" never sounded or felt right to me, but I was new, and I was eager to cooperate, so George Kerris it was . . . temporarily.

I never knew how or why, but super-producer Joe Pasternak saw my screen test and asked Paramount to loan me out to MGM for a small role in his movie *Meet Me in Las Vegas*, starring Cyd Charisse. Sweet and lovely Betty Lynn and I played a young married couple down on our luck in Vegas with no place to stay. At the end of a song we did with Cyd's co-star Dan Dailey called "It's Fun to Be in Love," he gave us the key to his hotel room. Legendary choreographer Hermes Pan, who had famously worked many times with Fred Astaire, staged "It's Fun to Be in Love." Maybe this George Kerris thing wasn't such a bad idea after all.

With Betty Lynn

As an added bonus, every time I passed Joe Pasternak on the lot, he'd greet me with a big smile and an enthusiastic, "You're going to be a big star! A *big* star!"

After I finished my work on the film I was allowed to keep driving on to the lot through the guarded MGM gate and wander around wherever I wanted. "Wherever I wanted" in this case was the *Meet Me in Las Vegas* soundstage, to watch Cyd Charisse perform the Sleeping Beauty ballet for that movie. She was partnered by Mark Wilder, a wonderful dancer and one of Jack Cole's favorites. He was as handsome as Cyd was beautiful. They were sublime together, and I was unapologetically their biggest fan.

I had a used but nice-looking gray Oldsmobile convertible by then. I was routinely waved through the MGM gate like I was Somebody. I had a Cyd Charisse movie coming out in a few months, and no less than Joe Pasternak was predicting stardom for me. George Kerris was feeling pretty good about himself.

On Cyd's last day of shooting the Sleeping Beauty ballet I parked my car and was headed toward the soundstage when I happened to run into Joe Pasternak's associate producer.

We chatted a bit; and then, just as we were heading to our respective destinations, he tossed in, almost as an afterthought, "Oh, by the way, the movie is running long, so we're going to have to cut your number." And off he went.

My heart hit the cement. With one "by the way," so much for my Cyd Charisse movie. So much for what suddenly felt like guilt-assuaging compliments from Joe Pasternak. Most of all, in that split second, in my mind, so much for George Kerris. My name was George Chakiris from then on, "commercial" or not, ethnic or not, no apologies, take it or leave it.

Paramount loaned me out to MGM several times, and I was so grateful. There were more movies and more brilliantly talented people. There were also dynamics going on at Paramount that none of us contract players could control. For one thing, the vast majority of producers who were making movies at that studio were independent, and they weren't obligated to use the studio's contract players. For another thing, by the mid-1950s, fewer movie musicals were being made, and this relatively new fad called television was giving audiences the option of not having to go to theaters anymore to be entertained.

So I can't honestly say I was surprised, or even all that disappointed, when a year after I signed with Paramount, they exercised their option to let me go. In fact, it freed me up for an opportunity I wouldn't have missed for anything.

It was 1956 when I got a call from my favorite choreographer Robert Alton. He and his trusty assistant, the wonderful Joan Bayley, were about to choreograph Judy Garland's Las Vegas debut at the New Frontier Hotel on the Strip.

The anticipation and excitement level for this show were off the charts, and Judy was about to become the highest-paid performer in Vegas history. Bob had hired eleven male chorus dancers for the four-week run and asked me to assist and work with the male dancers—Bob would teach me their choreography, and I would teach them.

If I hadn't been available, I would have *made* myself available.

And to dramatically understate it, they were four unforgettable weeks.

There are performers whose work can leave you in awe but who end up being a disappointment when you meet them. Judy Garland was *not* one of those performers. She was fascinating to be around. She was one of those people who made you feel she could see right through you. There wasn't a trace of pretense about her. For rehearsals she usually wore black tights and a man-tailored shirt. On opening night it became clear that she preferred the company of the behind-the-scenes people to the Hollywood celebrity crowd. I heard from several people that when she was working on films, she would deliberately fumble scenes at the end of the day, not to exasperate the executives but to make sure the crew and the dancers would work later than scheduled and add some overtime to their paychecks. She was very funny, not above telling some very off-color jokes with some very off-color language, and an extraordinary raconteur.

Bob Alton had worked with Judy at MGM on such classic musicals as *Easter Parade* with Fred Astaire and *The Harvey Girls* with Ray Bolger, Angela Lansbury, and a young, spectacular Cyd Charisse. Judy trusted

Bob completely, and he'd learned a couple of valuable things about her that came in very handy when preparing her Vegas show. For one thing, she was as natural at movement as she was at singing, which he used to fantastic advantage while choreographing for her. For another thing, she didn't much care for rehearsing. She was a flawlessly instinctive performer and artist, and she learned very quickly. Her album *Judy* had just been released, so the vast majority of our rehearsals were accompanied by Judy's album, played on a record player, with Joan Bayley standing in for Judy. One day Judy invited a few of us to her home so we could hear the album on a first-rate sound system, rather than on the little speakers on that record player at the L.A. dance studio where we rehearsed before going to Vegas. She was proud of that album, as she should have been, and she cared what we thought of it.

When Judy did rehearse, she tended to just "mark it" and quietly sing along with the recorded music. During one of those rehearsals, Joan whispered to Bob, "When is she going to *do* it?" To which Bob simply replied, "Just wait."

"Just wait." Exactly. Judy going from singing along with "Come Rain or Come Shine" on her album in half-voice to full-blown performing it was like going from a dimly lit room to the middle of a 4th of July fireworks display. She held back nothing when she performed, and no one connected more deeply to their material than Judy Garland did. Judy's daughter came to rehearsals a few times—adorable ten-year-old Liza Minnelli, always in darling little outfits and patent leather shoes, with her mama's huge, expressive eyes. Liza was very curious about what we were rehearsing and eager to learn. I taught her a few of the chorus dancers' combinations, which she picked up in the blink of an eye. Even then, in 1956, it was obvious that there was something very special going on in that child, who already had some dazzling inherited instincts.

Opening night was insane, packed beyond standing-room-only with what seemed like every celebrity in Hollywood, and you could have cut the excitement in the air with a knife, exactly as expected from Judy Garland live in Las Vegas. The opening number, "You're All Invited," was special material created by the great composer/arranger Roger Edens. It started with the eleven chorus guys coming out onstage carrying poles with placards on the top, each of them bearing a letter of the alphabet. As they danced into various positions they spelled out different words, like "Jaguar" and "Dandy" and "Lady" and "Jug Lad," until finally they spelled "Judy Garland," and out she came. The crowd roared and kept right on roaring all evening, after every perfect, magical song and God only knows how many encores and curtain calls. It was an unforgettable night and an unforgettable four weeks, and I headed back to L.A. gratified and very, very thankful.

I got to work for Bob Alton again in 1957, on a live TV special called *A Salute to Cole Porter*. Live television. No missing your cue, no retakes, no drawing a blank, just keep going and make it work no matter what happens. Terrifying, and indescribably exciting.

In the TV special *A Salute to Cole Porter*, 1954

The first performer on that special was Dorothy Dandridge, a fantastic musical talent and a superb actress, with a well-deserved Academy Award nomination for Otto Preminger's *Carmen Jones*. I'd watched all the rehearsals for the show and knew the numbers the different stars were doing. Dorothy did "My Heart Belongs to Daddy," and she was just magnificent. I did notice that during the number she made a tiny mistake and covered it so expertly that the audience would never have noticed. But I noticed. Seeing her make that small mistake unnerved me momentarily. What if I made a mistake? On live TV? Could I handle it as gracefully as she did? As her performance went on, though, I became so focused that the possibility of losing my way disappeared, and I was fine.

I'd been hired to partner a beautiful, accomplished actress/dancer named Sally Forrest.

Gordon MacRae, Shirley Jones, George Sanders, Dolores Gray, Louis Armstrong, all of us performing incomparable Cole Porter songs. Sally and I did two of them—"Begin the Beguine," and "Night and Day," which I got to sing. Again, live television! Like the theater, but even more pressure, and thrilling to do. Just thrilling.

With Sally Forrest in *A Salute to Cole Porter*, 1954

In the finale, all the stars gathered to welcome, in person, the frail, diminutive, impossibly brilliant Cole Porter himself. I stood on the sidelines, not joining the rest of the group, because I wasn't a star. But then someone came over and got me and pulled me onto the set with everyone else . . . and Cole Porter! What an honor that was.

I got great reviews for that special—so great that I took out two full-page ads, one in *Variety* and one in the *Hollywood Reporter*, with quotes from those reviews.

All of which led to . . . absolutely nothing.

And work for dancers in L.A. was continuing to fade right along with the production of movie musicals.

I'd been very blessed and very lucky, but I was starting to feel I was getting nowhere, running in place.

Finally, not discouraged, just following my instincts and the lead of several fellow chorus dancers, I said goodbye to my friends and my fantastic, supportive family, packed my bags and, in the summer of 1958, bought a one-way ticket to New York.

In "Tropicana Holiday Revue" starring Jayne Mansfield at the Tropicana Hotel Las Vegas, 1958

Chapter Three

MY FRIEND DRUSILLA DAVIS HAD ALREADY MOVED TO NEW YORK AND was sharing an apartment with a terrific friend named Marianne Mackay. I took them up on their generous invitation to camp out on their living room sofa and settled in for a crash course on making a living as a dancer in a tough new city.

Drusilla had already made the rounds and connected with people in the East Coast dance community, and Marianne happened to be working for the esteemed producer Roger L. Stevens. Between the two of them, there was nothing they didn't know about what was going on in the New York theater world.

The hottest musical in town was *West Side Story*. It had been a huge hit on Broadway for a year, and one night the three of us went to the Winter Garden Theater to see it. I was completely blown away by it. Carol Lawrence as Maria. Larry Kert as Tony. Ken LeRoy as Bernardo. Michael Callan as Riff. The incredible Chita Rivera, whom I'd idolized since my days at the American School of Dance, as Anita. Directed and choreographed by Jerome Robbins. Music and lyrics by Leonard Bernstein and Stephen Sondheim. Just electrifying, everywhere you turned.

So when Marianne mentioned that auditions were being held for the London production of *West Side Story* and strongly suggested I try to audition, I was thrilled at the thought! I would love to audition for that show, along with every other unemployed dancer in New York. Just point me to where they were lining up and I'd be happy to go stand in that line for as long as it took.

Well, no need to stand in line with friends like Dru and Marianne.

"Go to the stage door of the Winter Garden Theater and ask for Ruth Mitchell," Marianne told me. "She's the stage manager."

Done. I was off to the stage door of the Winter Garden Theater.

I'll never know if it was pure coincidence or some kind of cosmic sign, but the first person I ran into at the Winter Garden stage door wasn't Ruth Mitchell. It was a friend named Howard Jeffrey, whom I knew from the American School of Dance in Hollywood, where he'd been a star student.

"Howie!"

"George!"

Howard, it turned out, had made the move to New York a few years earlier, and he'd done very well for himself. He had been in Ballet Theatre—and he was now assisting choreographer Jerome Robbins on *West Side Story*.

After a few minutes of catching up, he had no problem understanding why I had come to the stage door. He promptly introduced me to stage manager Ruth Mitchell, briefly explaining how we knew each other and that we were friends.

She couldn't have been nicer, and I'm sure I had Howard's endorsement to thank for what happened next: She handed me a copy of the *West Side Story* script and told me to study the role of Bernardo, leader of the Sharks gang, for the upcoming London production.

"You'll be auditioning for Jerry [Jerome Robbins] in about a week. He's rehearsing Ballets: U.S.A. at the Alvin Theatre, so you'll read for him there." Once I'd convinced myself that yes, I had heard her correctly, I was going to be auditioning for *West Side Story*, I practically ran back to the apartment to tell Dru and Marianne the news and start working on that script. Now that I'd seen the Broadway production, I knew what a major, exciting challenge the role of Bernardo would be; I studied very hard that week.

The word on the street was that Jerome Robbins could be extremely difficult to work for but that it was always, *always* worth it. I'd seen his choreography with my own eyes. There was no doubt about it, the man was brilliant. A genius. And I really wanted this job.

So after a week of intensive studying and worrying and doing battle with my insecurities, I arrived at the door of the Alvin Theatre right on schedule, took a long, deep breath, walked inside . . . and found myself being welcomed by a friendly, gracious Jerome Robbins. He was pleasant. He was encouraging. He seemed to be happy to see me, and he had a fantastic, infectious smile. Okay. Good reminder that you can't believe everything you hear.

I read with the stage manager for the role of Bernardo, the Sharks' gang leader. I hoped it had gone well. But then, instead of the usual "thanks, good job, nice meeting you, we'll be in touch" at the end of the audition, Jerry threw me a curve—he asked me to go back in the wings, study the script for twenty minutes or so, and let him hear me read for the role of Riff, leader of the Sharks' rival gang, the Jets.

I did, and that went well too, well enough that when I finished, Jerry handed me the sheet music for "Cool," a number Riff sings in *West Side Story*.

"Learn it, work on it, and I'll see you again in about ten days."

I really liked this man. I wanted so much to work for him. And "Cool" was a fantastic number. I hired a pianist, immersed myself in preparing for that audition, and was back onstage at the Alvin Theatre ten days later, singing "Cool" for Jerome Robbins.

I never had to dance for Jerry. It turns out he had seen *Salute to Cole Porter*, and that was enough for him to trust me as a dancer. So *Salute to Cole Porter* was helpful after all, and working for Robert Alton helped me with Jerry Robbins.

After the audition I went back to the apartment to wait, which, as everyone in this business will agree, is one of the biggest challenges in the profession. While the phone kept not ringing, I got curious about where *West Side Story* came from in the first place, and why it was common knowledge that once upon a time, during the many years it took to become a reality, it was widely considered to be "doomed," "impossible," "too dark and depressing," and "a guaranteed artistic flop."

The evolution of what eventually became known as "the best-loved musical of all time" was a long, fascinating, uphill journey. I couldn't help but think of what was going on in my life while *West Side Story* was struggling its way into existence, and how easy it is to forget that sometimes things happen in this world we know nothing about, until they cross our paths and change everything.

It seems that in 1947, when I was a thirteen-year-old boy in Long Beach, singing with the St. Luke's Choristers, sneaking off to the movies and dreaming of being a part of them, Jerome Robbins was sitting down in his New York apartment one night with Leonard Bernstein and Arthur Laurents to discuss his idea of doing a musical version of a modern-day *Romeo and Juliet*.

In Jerry's vision, the Shakespearian classic would take place in the slums of Manhattan's Lower East Side. It would be centered around a conflict between a Catholic gang, the Jets, and a Jewish gang, the Emeralds, during the Easter-Passover season. Against that backdrop, the tragedy of the two star-crossed lovers, a member of the Catholic gang (Romeo) and an Israeli girl who'd survived the Holocaust (Juliet) would unfold. The title of the work would be *East Side Story*.

Arthur Laurents, a well-established playwright and screenwriter, had been looking forward to writing his first musical. He saw the potential of Jerry's concept and signed on. And Leonard Bernstein had been wanting to resuscitate grand musical theater, even opera, in America, with a modern twist that would appeal to a non-classical audience. *East Side Story* sounded like it might be an opportunity to realize that ambition. Robbins and Laurents weren't especially enthusiastic about the idea of trying to sell a grand musical theater/opera concept on the Broadway stage, but they temporarily tabled that discussion until the project progressed a little further.

Laurents wrote a first draft of the script. Second thoughts set in, though, about the possibility that it was too soon after World War II to even touch the still-very-sensitive issue of anti-Semitism. Then Laurents, Robbins, and Bernstein all found themselves needing to focus on other work commitments; and by mid-1949, while I was attending high school and falling in love with dancing and Joan Scanlon, *East Side Story* was shelved until the creators were available to revisit it and decide whether or not it was worth pursuing.

It wasn't until six years later, in 1955, that the subject of the abandoned project came up again. Robbins, Laurents, and Bernstein had reunited for a stage adaptation of the James M. Cain novel *Serenade*, which never happened. Inevitably, they began talking about *East Side Story*. One of the hurdles they were facing by then was the fact that Leonard Bernstein had become overwhelmed by the thought of writing both the music and the lyrics for the score. As luck would have it, Arthur Laurents had been introduced to a young songwriter named Stephen Sondheim and suggested he write the lyrics for Bernstein's *East Side Story* score. Sondheim was reluctant at first, but after talking to his mentor Oscar Hammerstein, he finally decided to say yes.

After *Serenade* fell through, Laurents moved on to a screenplay for a film in Hollywood. Leonard Bernstein happened to be in Los Angeles at the same time, conducting a concert at the Hollywood Bowl. The two of them got together at the Beverly Hills Hotel, a few miles from MGM where I was working on *Meet Me in Las Vegas* with Cyd Charisse and Dan Dailey. Laurents and Bernstein found themselves discussing the headline in the morning *Los Angeles Times* about the eruption of a violent Chicano gang turf war, which led to a brief conversation about reworking *East Side Story* with the theme of a Mexican-American gang conflict and setting it in L.A.

Laurents, though, wasn't comfortable with that idea—he wasn't nearly as familiar with Los Angeles as he was with Manhattan, where dramatic changes had taken place since he wrote the first draft of *East Side Story* six years earlier. The Lower East Side slums had been demolished, and more than half a million Puerto Ricans had moved to New York and radically changed the cultural makeup of its population.

From that meeting between Laurents and Bernstein at the Beverly Hills Hotel, and the transformations taking place in New York City's ethnic breakdown, the original Catholic/Jewish concept of *East Side Story* evolved into a racial conflict instead. The warring factions were reconceived as a Puerto Rican gang, the Sharks, vs. the white gang, the Jets. "Romeo" became Tony, a Polish-Irish former member of the Jets. "Juliet" became Maria, the Puerto Rican sister of the Sharks' leader Bernardo.

Leonard Bernstein loved Latin rhythms, and Latin music was very popular in the mid-1950s; so Bernstein's historic score became an inspired bridge between the Jets' American jazz-blues and the Sharks' Puerto Rican pitch-percussion Latin American theme. Stephen Sondheim's incomparable lyrics were added to the score, and the title of the redevised project was finally changed to *West Side Story*.

Backers' auditions began in the spring of 1957, while I was busy in L.A. doing the Cole Porter live TV special. They were a disaster. No one wanted to invest in a Broadway show that featured a dark score, gang fights, and three murders, particularly at a time when Broadway was thriving with feel-good musicals like *The Merry Widow*, *My Fair Lady*, *Damn Yankees*, and *Guys and Dolls*. It didn't help that the talented cast presented to the potential backers—Carol Lawrence, Michael Callan, Ken LeRoy, Larry Kert, et al.—were relative unknowns. Producer Cheryl Crawford pulled out six weeks before rehearsals were scheduled to start, convinced that *West Side Story* was destined to fail.

Robbins, Bernstein, Laurents, and Sondheim were understandably depressed and discouraged. Maybe their detractors were right. Maybe their creation, and the ten years of hard work and dedication they'd put into it, really was doomed after all. Maybe it was time to give it up, take the loss, and move on.

On a last-minute Hail Mary impulse, Stephen Sondheim reached out to Tony Award-winning producer Hal Prince, who was just beginning to establish himself as a major theatrical giant. Prince read the script, liked it, and agreed to listen to the score. As he remembered in his autobiography, "Sondheim and Bernstein sat at the piano playing through the music, and soon I was singing along with them." He signed on and began cutting the budget and raising money.

Finally, on September 26, 1957, a full house that included Marlene Dietrich, Cary Grant, and Tyrone Power crowded into the Winter Garden Theater at 1634 Broadway to witness the opening night of *West Side Story*, the "impossible" "guaranteed artistic flop" no one believed in.

When the show ended, there was dead silence when the curtain went up for the curtain call. Then, a beat later, the audience leapt to its feet, applauding and cheering through an astonishing seventeen curtain calls.

West Side Story was still a massive hit almost a year later, when I followed my instinct to move to New York and was sent by my friends Dru and Marianne to the stage door of the Winter Garden Theater. At exactly the right moment to run into my old friend Howard Jeffrey. Which led to my introduction to Ruth Mitchell. Which led to my auditioning for

Jerome Robbins, the man who'd planted the seeds of West Side Story to begin with.

And then, on September 16, 1958, my twenty-fourth birthday, seven unemployment checks for $35 apiece arrived from California . . . and Ruth Mitchell called to congratulate me— Jerome Robbins was officially offering me the role of Riff in the London production of *West Side Story*.

After learning about the show's remarkable history, I wasn't just happy to have the job. I wasn't just grateful to Jerome Robbins for hiring me. I wasn't just excited to be part of a brilliant musical that had come so close to never existing. I was honored.

When my new castmates and I gathered for our first day of rehearsals on the Winter Garden Theater stage, the nervous excitement in the air was palpable. We were eager, we were anxious, and we all had one thing in common as we introduced ourselves to each other—we knew we'd earned being there, but we still couldn't quite believe it.

Jerry began the morning by having the Sharks and the Jets assemble onstage. Then he planted himself in front of us and announced, "Okay, we've got three weeks to do this, so let's get to work. I want the Sharks over here [he pointed stage left] and the Jets over there [he pointed stage right]." He then made it very clear that he didn't want the Sharks and the Jets socializing with each other before, during, or after rehearsals.

I've always thought that was so smart of him. For one thing, he was working with a bunch of relatively inexperienced young people and making it clear who was in charge. For another thing, it was an inspired way to help create the tension between the two rival gangs that he needed from us onstage. That tension is essential. Without it, *West Side Story* just plain doesn't work. And to deepen our understanding of the underlying territorial, combative mentality of the Sharks and the Jets, he insisted that we all read a book about juvenile delinquency that came out earlier that year, *The Shook-Up Generation* by Harrison Evans Salisbury. Jerry demanded depth and authenticity from us, and we loved him for it.

Those three weeks of rehearsals at the Winter Garden were brutally challenging. I was completely overwhelmed. I left the theater exhausted every day, thinking, *I'm never going to learn all this*. But the alternative was *not* learning it and being replaced, and no way did I want that to happen.

I knew I was launching into a once-in-a-lifetime opportunity, and I desperately wanted to be up to the task.

Somehow, three weeks later, ready or not, we gave our first performance, for an audience made up of the Broadway community. No pressure there.

But we had an extraordinary cast, we'd worked hard, and we had an ace in the hole—Chita Rivera, the force of nature who'd originated the role of Anita in the *West Side Story* Broadway cast, was joining us in the London production. She was spectacular that night, personally and professionally. The show went beautifully, the audience of our peers was fantastically enthusiastic, and we were off to an amazing start.

In what seemed like the blink of an eye, we were all on a chartered plane—the cast, the crew, Jerry, his assistant and my old friend Howard Jeffrey, Arthur Laurents, Hal Prince, Stephen Sondheim, everyone but Leonard Bernstein—headed to Manchester, England, for rehearsals and our pre-London engagement at the historic Opera House on November 14, 1958.

Without exception, the people of Manchester were warm, welcoming, and absolutely lovely. The city itself, on the other hand, was perpetually dark and shrouded in a thick, pervasive, pea-soup fog. Chita's husband, dancer/choreographer Tony Mordente, who was cast as A-Rab in the London production, was so inspired by the foggy atmosphere that he insisted on playing relentless Frankenstein pranks on us for the duration of our stay there. A point came where we almost worried about him if ten minutes went by when he wasn't leaping out at us from behind a door or some nearby tree!

I woke up one morning for an 11:00 a.m. rehearsal and thanks to the pea-soup fog thought it was still the middle of the night. I came to my senses in time to arrive at the theater several minutes early and find Hal Prince being interviewed by the press in the orchestra pit.

I didn't overhear much, and I'm sure he didn't intend for me or any other member of the cast to overhear him when he told them, "Pay no attention to anyone in the show. Just focus on the show itself."

Now, there's a real confidence-builder from your producer—ignore all those people you'll see onstage knocking themselves out night after night, the only star here worth focusing on is *West Side Story*. And good luck convincing people to pay no attention to anyone in the show when you've got Chita Rivera onstage.

It never occurred to me to say anything to Hal about what I'd heard, but obviously I didn't appreciate it. Then again, Hal did have a reputation for being abrasive. One of the many popular, often-quoted sayings about him was, "Hal Prick is a Prince." So it wasn't easy, but eventually I learned to shrug off thoughtless remarks like that one as just Hal being Hal. And in the end, what difference would it really make anyway? The press and our audiences would make up their own minds about *West Side Story*, no matter what Hal Prince had to say.

To the surprise of no one but maybe Hal, Manchester loved us—the show *and* the cast. We were thrilled at how well received we were and what fantastic momentum we had when we moved on to London.

Chapter Four

WEST SIDE STORY OPENED IN LONDON AT HER MAJESTY'S THEATRE ON December 12, 1958. Jerry fired up the cast with an inspiring pep talk before the performance, and we were on fire when we hit the stage that night. There wasn't an empty seat in the house, and we were rewarded with a wildly enthusiastic standing ovation and more curtain calls than I could count.

First day in London, 1958

After the show we all put on our best formal wear and gathered at the Savoy to celebrate and wait for the reviews to come in. As if we weren't already a distinguished enough group, we were joined by what seemed like everyone in the prestigious London theater crowd, including none other than Sir Nöel Coward. The reviews were raves, and I gaped when I saw that the two performers they singled out most were Chita and me.

Marlys Waters ("Maria") and Noel Coward on opening night of *West Side Story* in London, 1958

We did a special performance of *West Side Story* for Queen Elizabeth's sister, Princess Margaret, before opening night. We had the honor of meeting her backstage, and I remember how flawlessly beautiful she was, with a perfect porcelain complexion.

By the time we got to London I'd made friends with castmate David Bean, who played Tiger, one of the Jets. David's godfather was the much-beloved British actor Cyril Ritchard. Cyril was fresh from his Tony Award-winning performance as Mr. Darling and the villainous Captain Hook in the Mary Martin Broadway production of *Peter Pan*. He of course knew Jerry—it was Jerry who staged and directed all of *Peter Pan*. In fact, he knew everyone in London, and everyone in London knew and adored him. He was a lovely and generous man. Thanks to Cyril and his connections, David and I found ourselves renting a fantastic mews house with a prestigious address, 13 Eccleston Mews just off Eaton Square.

Meeting Princess Margaret backstage at Her Majesty's Theater, London, 1958

All of which is to explain the occasional flashes I had of looking around at my life and thinking I must be dreaming.

The only downside of those early days and nights in London was the result of my own negligence.

When we were in rehearsals in New York before we left for England, Jerry warned me to wear body pads while we rehearsed the very physical rumble between Riff and Bernardo. I didn't listen. To Jerome Robbins. I got badly bruised, and by the time we opened in London, I was in so much pain from the bruises that it kept me awake, night after night after night.

On stage as Riff in the London company production
of *West Side Story*, 1959

With fellow Jet David Bean in the London company of *West Side Story*, 1959

There was a relatively new medication on the market at the time that was said to be a very effective anti-insomnia treatment. It was called Doriden, and a few friends highly recommended it. I headed off to the chemist and picked some up to try, and what do you know, it helped. A lot. So much so that I kept right on buying it and right on taking it. It never occurred to me to stop when the bruises had healed, and in my defense, no one ever suggested I should. It still amazes me to look back and realize how naïve and uninformed society and I were about drugs in general and Doriden in particular back then—no prescription necessary, no warnings, if it worked it worked, what a relief, always keep plenty on hand. By the time more was known about this "safe alternative to barbiturates," I'd become addicted.

I stayed addicted for many, many years to what the FDA ultimately classified as a Schedule II drug, a hypnotic sedative "with a high potential for abuse." It ultimately took two very helpful weeks in a hospital in Laguna Beach, California, for me to get clean of Doriden and stay that way.

Or, I could have simply taken Jerry's advice and worn body pads in the first place.

I fell in love with London the moment we arrived. Somehow, even though I'd never been there before, it immediately felt like home, like I belonged there. The English nature was very much like mine. And one of the countless joys of being introduced to it as part of the cast in a hit show was being embraced by the London theater community and welcomed into its gracious, busy social life.

Chita and her husband Tony had a beautiful three-story house in Chelsea. They rented rooms there to the fabulously hilarious Yvonne Othon Wilder (our Teresita and Chita's understudy) and to Riggs O'Hara, who played Snowboy, one of the Jets. That house became one of our favorite places to laugh and decompress after a performance. When we weren't there, or at a popular watering hole called The Buxton, we were accepting invitations from a long list of extraordinary people in their extraordinary homes for Sunday lunch and after-hours parties.

Suddenly, there I was, hanging out with actors from the esteemed Royal Court Theatre in Sloane Square. George Devine. Lindsay Anderson, who asked me to choreograph *The Lilywhite Boys* with Albert Finney and Shirley Anne Field. The utterly incandescent Jill Bennett. A couple of charismatic rising stars named Peter O'Toole and Albert Finney. Not just hanging out with them, but trading stories with them and feeling like one of their peers. I hid it as best I could, but more than once I found myself feeling like that awestruck young boy visiting MGM Studios for the first time with the St. Luke's Choristers, almost having to fight back tears of grateful disbelief at where my life had taken me.

I even worked up the courage—or maybe the colossal lack of good manners—to knock on Julie Andrews's Eaton Square door on Christmas Eve, not because I was invited but because I knew Chita was a guest at a party there. Julie graciously welcomed me. Chita and the rest of the glittering houseful of guests acted as if they'd been expecting me and were hoping I'd show up. Exhilarating as it was, I still cringe a little looking back on it, wondering what possessed me to be so presumptuous that night, and to Julie Andrews of all people!

I became especially close friends with an irresistible British actress named Fanny Carby. Knowing Fanny was one of the joys of my life, and it seemed as if all of London felt exactly the same way about her. She was invited everywhere, and she invited me to go everywhere with her. She became a great friend for life. On one of our more memorable Sunday afternoons we went to a casual gathering at the Abbey Road home of entertainment journalist Peter Noble and his wife, actress Marianne Stone.

One of the first guests we noticed, because it was impossible not to, was Diana Dors, Great Britain's answer to Marilyn Monroe. She was all about glamour, draped across a chaise lounge in a black velvet gown and long, silky, platinum-blonde hair, beautifully manicured nails, and her big black Cadillac with its fins and its personalized "DD" license plate waiting for her outside. It was such a pleasant surprise to discover how nice and "human" she was under all that effort. But mostly, I remember that as Fanny and I were leaving, I noticed a guy sitting all by himself in the Nobles' impeccably manicured backyard. He was turned away from the house with a drink in his hand, and he clearly wanted to be left alone.

I felt badly for him and pointed him out to Fanny.

"Oh, that's poor Sean," she said. "He can't seem to find work."

He turned out to be "poor Sean" Connery. He found work.

It still makes me smile to think of one night after a performance when the legendary London fog was so thick you couldn't see ten feet ahead of you. A cab was out of the question. David and I had to walk home to Eccleston Mews literally feeling our way along and hoping we were on the right street. We really were guessing. It was very slow!

My social life was briefly interrupted—and believe me, I wasn't complaining—by rehearsals for a gala called *Night of 100 Stars*, being hosted by Sir Laurence Olivier. Someone came up with the idea of including "those two guys from *West Side Story*," i.e., Bernardo and Riff, aka Ken LeRoy and me, in the show. The question was how to use us.

The producers came up with an idea Ken and I both loved. They teamed us with a terrific British actress/dancer named Elizabeth Seal, who was starring in *Irma La Douce* in the West End's Lyric Theatre, and the three of us performed the Bob Fosse "Steam Heat" number from *The Pajama Game*. Ken had done *The Pajama Game* on Broadway and knew the number inside out. Fantastic. Classic Fosse. Ken, Elizabeth, and I

In my dressing room at Her Majesty's Theater, London, 1959

wore matching suits and bowler hats, and Fosse had *really* worked those hats into the movement. We rehearsed like crazy and had a great time, except for the pervasive, nerve-wracking fear of dropping our hats during the countless hat tricks Fosse had created.

The performance went perfectly, without a single drop of the hat, to a very appreciative audience that included Audrey Hepburn, Laurence Harvey, and the most talked-about star of the evening, my old MGM schoolmate, none other than the insanely gorgeous Elizabeth Taylor.

Elizabeth was there with her new husband Eddie Fisher, trying with steely defiance to ignore the global disdain that was currently surrounding her in the press for breaking up the marriage of "America's Sweethearts," Eddie Fisher and Debbie Reynolds. Elizabeth sat in the front row and beamed up at Eddie like a dutiful newlywed while he sang two songs:

"You Are Too Beautiful," and "They All Laughed." I've always wondered who selected those songs for him that night.

After more than a year of performances and spectacular London hospitality, we started hearing that *West Side Story* was going to be made into a movie.

Needless to say, this started a nonstop frenzy of rumors and speculation among the cast. Would that movie include any of us? If not, who would it include? There was a bulletin board at the theater, and it seemed as if every day there was some new real or imagined update posted there.

The first casting possibility we heard was Elvis Presley for the role of Tony. According to the rumor mill and the bulletin board, United Artists and the Mirisch Brothers, who were producing the *West Side Story* movie, had already approached Elvis about it. But in the end, his manager Colonel Tom Parker turned it down.

Once Elvis was out of the running, they were considering Robert Redford, Burt Reynolds, Tab Hunter, Warren Beatty, Russ Tamblyn. . . . They reportedly decided that Russ Tamblyn wasn't right for Tony, but they liked him and agreed to keep him in mind in case some other appropriate role came along.

The first contender they discussed to play Maria was Elizabeth Taylor. They'd tested Carol Lawrence as a possibility to reprise her great run as Maria on Broadway. Too old, they eventually agreed—even though she was actually six months younger than Elizabeth. It's that kind of business. But hey, Elizabeth Taylor was Elizabeth Taylor, so how could they *not* consider her? And if she didn't work out, maybe Jane Fonda, or Audrey Hepburn, or Suzanne Pleshette. . . .

Then one day, according to the story he himself told many times, Robert Wise screened some footage from the recently completed movie *Splendor in the Grass* to get a long, close look at Warren Beatty for Tony. Next thing he knew, he'd forgotten all about Warren Beatty—he couldn't take his eyes off of Warren's co-star in that film, a beautiful ingenue named Natalie Wood. After that screening he announced, "That's our Maria."

In the meantime, the more those movie star names appeared on the bulletin board, the more resigned we London cast members became to the probability that we didn't stand a chance of being cast in the film version of *West Side Story* . . . until one day when, out of nowhere, five of us got letters from United Artists asking us to test for it.

We couldn't believe it. As many times as we'd heard of yet another big name being considered for yet another major role in the movie and thought, "Well, so much for us," there was always that tiny shred of hope. And now, that tiny shred seemed to be growing. Suddenly we weren't exactly confident, but we were cautiously euphoric.

There was just one thing dampening my enthusiasm. My letter asked me to prepare two scenes for the test: one as Riff, and one as Bernardo. My first thought was, "I don't want to play Bernardo." I'd been playing Riff for a year and a half. I loved that character. I knew Riff inside out. Of course, after a year and a half, I pretty much knew every character in *West Side Story* inside out. I could probably have played Anita or Baby John by then without a single rehearsal. But Riff had become very personal to me.

Besides, Ken LeRoy had played Bernardo on Broadway, and he was playing Bernardo in London. Ken wasn't unfriendly, he just didn't seem to be a "group" person, and he was a fantastic Bernardo. He'd also told me once, when he and I were privately rehearsing the war council scene, "You're going to win an Academy Award." I shrugged it off, but it was such a generous, unexpected compliment . . . about my portrayal of Riff. Not Bernardo.

Then again, if United Artists wanted a scene as Riff and a scene as Bernardo, that's of course what I had to do. Once they saw the test, they'd be able to figure out on their own that I was obviously meant to play Riff. How else could this possibly go? (For the record, I've never claimed that these instincts I've relied on so often are 100 percent accurate.)

On the appointed day, the five of us who'd received those letters from United Artists were driven to the Elstree Studios outside of London to shoot our screen tests—Ken LeRoy, Riggs O'Hara, Yvonne Wilder, David Bean, and I. I wore Ken LeRoy's costume for my test as Bernardo, and I remember thinking when I was doing my Riff scene that the lighting wasn't good for any of us. I knew that a strong overhead light didn't help anyone, and I was right. The first thing director Robert Wise said to me when I eventually met him was, "We're going to have to do something about the bags under your eyes." (I was twenty-seven. I swear I didn't have those.) After a long, exciting, intensely focused eight hours at the Elstree Studios, we drove back to the theater on a full-blown adrenaline high that lasted through our performances at the theater that night and beyond.

Then, of course, days went by. Weeks went by. The silence from United Artists and the Mirisch Brothers was deafening. As we passed each other in the halls of the theater every night, we kept asking each other, "Have you heard anything?" None of us had. Nothing. Not a word.

At about the five- or six-week mark, we came to the unanimous conclusion that oh, well, so much for the movie version of *West Side Story*. At least we'd gotten a shot at it. It would have been great, but we still had our steady jobs doing the stage version we all loved. We were disappointed, but we could hardly complain.

Just under two months later I was in my dressing room getting ready to go onstage when I was called to the stage door phone. Jerry Robbins was calling.

"We like your test," he said, "but we'd like to test you further. Could you get a leave of absence for a week and come to L.A.?"

He didn't say what role they wanted to test me further for. I was so excited I didn't ask. The movie was still a possibility after all! And a trip to L.A. meant a chance to see my family and friends there for the first time in more than a year and a half.

The London company gave me the week's leave of absence, and I was on a plane to Los Angeles the next day.

It was great to give my father a big, long hug when he picked me up at LAX. I'd missed him so much! We drove to Goldwyn Studios the next day where Robert Wise and Jerry had their offices. I met Robert Wise for the first time, and he couldn't have been nicer. He explained that my screen test would happen on Thursday. Jerry would direct the test and I'd be testing for the role of Bernardo.

I was much too revved up to ask if Riff had been cast. Bernardo was the subject at hand, and that's of course what took my concentration. I tested with a really wonderful actress named Barbara Luna, whose self-confidence I wished I could bottle and sell. I felt and hoped the test had gone well. Jerry, perfectionist that he was, seemed pleased with it. It was so great to spend that time with him. I flew back to London on Sunday and was onstage for Monday night's performance, happy to be there and happy to be onstage playing Riff again. It all felt so good.

And then (feel free to say it along with me), more weeks of silence went by. To his credit, Robert Wise was enough of a gentleman to send me a letter at some point that said, "We're sorry we haven't let you know anything yet, but we feel we have to lock in the casting of Maria before we can finalize casting her brother."

Understandable. It didn't make the waiting any easier, but better that than a letter containing the typical rejection euphemism, "We've decided to go another way."

Again, I never lost sight of how lucky I was. I was performing *West Side Story*, a show I loved, live onstage, in London, a city I loved, surrounded by friends I loved.

But still, good God, did I want to be part of that movie!

More than a month went by.

I'd become a tennis fan while I was in living in England, and tennis didn't get any better than the two weeks at the end of June and the beginning of July, when the best of the best players in the world come to London for the Wimbledon Championships.

Some friends and I were at Wimbledon one afternoon, watching a match between Rod Laver and Alan Mills. All of a sudden, I can't explain it, I felt an urgent need to get to the theater ASAP. It made no sense—my call time was hours away, and I was a big Rod Laver fan. But it was too strong an impulse to ignore.

I was out of there in the middle of the match (Laver won, I found out later), raced through London to Her Majesty's Theatre, and sprinted to the stage door . . . where a telegram from Jerry Robbins was waiting for me.

Natalie Wood had officially signed on to play Maria in the film version of *West Side Story*, it said, and congratulations, I was being offered the role of her brother Bernardo.

To add to what I can only describe as pure joy, I soon found out that I wasn't the only member of the London cast being hired for the movie. David Bean would be reprising his London role of Tiger. Yvonne Wilder, Teresita in the London production, was cast as Consuelo, one of the Sharks' girls. Eddie Verso, our Baby John in London, would be Juano, a Shark. And Chita's husband Tony Mordente, A-Rab in London, would be playing Action, a Jet, in the movie.

It goes without saying that we were ecstatic; and it meant so much that our cast and understudies, who were like family by now, were ecstatic for us and wished us all the success in the world.

As grateful as I was to have been cast in the movie, and as excited as I was about it, I was going to miss sharing a stage with every one of those fantastic people.

Then again, I'd be back before too long—my role in the film version of *West Side Story* would only require me to be gone for ten weeks.

I was gone for eight months.

Chapter Five

THE PROLOGUE OF *WEST SIDE STORY* WAS SHOT IN NEW YORK CITY, ON 68th Street between Amsterdam and West End Avenue. The girls weren't involved in the prologue—it was just the guys, the Sharks and the Jets. We were housed at the Warwick Hotel, and I was so grateful to Bob Wise's assistant director Robert Relyea, who was in charge of room assignments, for honoring my request to have a room to myself. I certainly didn't want to be unfriendly; it's just my nature to be quiet, and private, and more comfortable alone at the end of the day, an important time to relax and think. Most of all, I knew that living up to Jerry's expectations for Bernardo was going to take all the concentration I could possibly give it.

Rehearsing the prologue with Jerry
Robbins, 1960

Jerry was never content with having his actors just know their lines and their dance steps. He expected every one of us to put thought into their character, who they were and why, where they came from, what they expected out of life, anything that would deepen the performance. One day while we were rehearsing for the London production, Jerry pulled me aside and asked, "Why do you think your character is called 'Riff'?" I have no idea what my answer was, if I had one at all. It had never even entered my mind to wonder about it. But I got his point: I was going to be assuming my character's identity for two hours a night, hopefully for a long time to come. Wouldn't it be a good idea to think about *who he is*? It was a profound and thought-provoking suggestion. I'd taken it to heart while I prepared to play Riff, and I was determined to make the same commitment while I prepared to play Bernardo.

ABOVE AND RIGHT: Getting a little coaching from Jerome Robbins on location in New York in 1960
UNITED ARTISTS/PHOTOFEST

Bright and early every morning the Sharks and the Jets would descend on the Warwick coffee shop, a very energetic and enthusiastic young group, wolfing down all the caffeine and doughnuts we could get our hands on and talking a mile a minute while we waited for the bus to show up and drive us to the location.

The prologue of *West Side Story*, of course, is the sequence at the beginning of the film when the Sharks and the Jets have their initial confrontation on the streets of New York. In my opinion, it's a perfect introduction to an extraordinary facet of Jerome Robbins's choreography: Jerry never choreographed a dance number that was simply a dance number. To him, all dance numbers were dialogue through movement, part of the storytelling rather than musical timeouts that put the storytelling on hold. He choreographed for character, and our work as dancers was part of our work as actors. So from the very beginning, we knew we were expected not just to perform our steps but to express what those steps and those moves meant. It wasn't always easy, but it was a gloriously creative way to work and perform.

Confronting the Jets in the opening scenes of *West Side Story*, 1960
UNITED ARTISTS/PHOTOFEST

We all arrived at the location for our first day of filming and started the morning with the rehearsals that would be a daily routine throughout shooting the movie. Then it was time to film the first shot of *West Side Story*—me, with my fist against the red brick wall. It only required a small group of us, just me, Jerry, Bob Wise, the camera crew, and our makeup man Emile LaVigne, all of them close around me on the set for the very tight, very intense shot. I loved how intimate and important it felt that we were so close together, and I could strongly sense Jerry's presence on the other side of the camera. As an actor, I understood what a powerful moment it was for Bernardo. Feeling Jerry's eyes laser-focused on me from just a few feet away helped me turn up the heat. I understood what he wanted from me, and I deeply hoped I was "getting it."

During a break while shooting the prologue I found myself standing next to Jerry. He was quiet. I was quiet. I didn't know what to say. He didn't know what to say. I realized he was just as shy as I was. The silence was broken by our being called back to work. Saved by the bell. I had such

George Chakiris

AFI is proud to recognize your outstanding performance in

WEST SIDE STORY

#41 America's 100 Greatest Movies

Chairman

Director and CEO

AFI

Advancing and preserving
the art of the moving image

respect for him, and I was so annoyed with myself for not managing to come up with something to say.

Years later, at a *West Side Story* screening at Paramount, Bob Relyea explained to the audience that the shot of me with my fist against the red brick wall was the first thing we filmed and the first rushes anyone had seen. "That shot of George made us all feel we 'had something,'" he told them, and it was so satisfying to know that the powerful excitement of shooting it had been accurately translated to the big screen.

I have to admit, I'd wondered before we started rehearsals if it would be strange to work opposite someone else playing Riff, after a year and a half of playing Riff myself. It wasn't. Not at all. I loved sharing scenes with Russ Tamblyn, and Russ made Riff *his*, spot-on from his first moment onscreen to his last. The confidence he brought to that role was infectious, and it was made even more remarkable by the fact that Russ was a trained gymnast. He kept hoping Jerry would work some acrobatics into the choreography. I'm not sure he was ever quite convinced that his dancing was on the same level as all the trained dancers around him, until Fred Astaire

The famous hand-on-wall shot at the opening of *West Side Story*
UNITED ARTISTS/PHOTOFEST

came up to him after a screening and complimented him on it. Praise from Fred Astaire on your dancing is as good as it gets, so congratulations, Russ, and take a beautifully deserved bow!

The Sharks and Jets didn't fraternize, at Jerry's wise request, but one-upmanship between the two gangs started as a playful competition we all loved and kind of organically evolved as the filming progressed.

The schoolyard and streets where we shot the prologue, for example, were surrounded by apartment buildings, and the residents would stand on their balconies to watch the filming. So courtesy of the Jets, we all arrived one morning to find a large banner hanging from one of those balcony railings that read "Sharks Stink!" The Sharks took that banner down as soon as they could reach that balcony!

Russ climbing the fire escape at 110th Street in New York to take down the Sharks banner

One day Andre Tayir, who played Chile, one of the Sharks, showed up at rehearsal wearing a black leather wristband. We loved it. Jerry loved it. Bob loved it. Our costume designer Irene Sharaff loved it. So black leather wristbands were promptly and secretly purchased by all the Sharks so that we could reveal them as a surprise show of strength against the Jets in the dance hall scene.

In that scene, the mambo segment is introduced by the Sharks. Jerry staged it for the Sharks, both the guys and the girls, to go into a huddle on one side of the stage. Coming out of the huddle, we all formed a diagonal line that moved across the floor of the gym. The first step of the mambo starts with the Sharks' right arms extended, palms forward in a sort of defiant, "in your face" salute with those matching wristbands on our wrists as we crossed in time with the music. It was a very strong visual and a symbolic show of strength from the Sharks to the Jets, both onscreen and off. That was an important moment for the Sharks and we loved it!

I still have my wristband, and I wouldn't part with it for anything. Thank you again, Andre!

The Jets never came up with anything to equal it, but they certainly tried. This ongoing, creative, harmless rivalry between the two gangs lasted for the duration of filming. We had a good time coming up with new ways to needle each other and keep that sense of tension between the gangs intact. And I'm convinced that part of the motivation behind Jerry's "no fraternizing between gangs" edict helped inspire another bonus of that rivalry—neither the Sharks nor the Jets were going to let the other gang out-dance them.

It was sweltering hot on the streets of New York when we shot the prologue, well over 100 degrees. Jerry's choreography was thrilling to perform. It was also intensely challenging and sometimes exhausting, especially in that heat, leaping and strutting and kicking and dancing our hearts out, up one block and down another. But we all had the feeling from the very beginning that we were working on something extraordinary, and every one of us gave it everything we had, hour after hour, day after day. Part of it was the professionalism in all of us. Another part of it was the determination, almost a survival instinct, to rise to the incredibly high level of Jerry's expectations. And we loved what we were doing!

It was a relief, and very satisfying, when Bob Wise finally announced one afternoon, "Okay! That was good! Cut and print!"

Now, the legend is that Bob's announcement was followed by an announcement from Jerry: "Actually, I'd like to do one more take, but this time I want all you Jets to do it on the other foot."

Some of the Jets remember it, and some of them don't. Russ swears it happened. We Sharks had wrapped for the day, so I wasn't there and can't say if it happened or not. If it did, Bob Wise, as the co-director, could have put a stop to it but obviously didn't. All I know is that "other foot" or not, by that night, Bob and Jerry were satisfied, the prologue was "in the can," and we were off to L.A. to film the rest of *West Side Story*.

I found another apartment in Hollywood with a street address that added up to seven, settled in, and started rehearsals at the Samuel Goldwyn Studios, where we'd be shooting. It was at that first rehearsal that I met Rita Moreno, Bernardo's love interest Anita in the movie, who's gone on to become a lifelong friend.

You don't need me to tell you that Rita's a knockout. I'm sure you've noticed. I noticed too, the minute I saw her. And that turned out to be only the beginning of what Rita Moreno had to offer. She was, and is, an unbelievably conscientious performer and actress. From Minute One of Day One, no one worked harder than she did. Anita was a very demanding role, especially for a woman who hadn't danced since she was sixteen, twelve years earlier, and Rita was fantastic, onscreen and off. She was playful, she was outspoken, she was focused, and she was funny. I went to lunch every day with her and the equally funny Yvonne Othon Wilder. Yvonne had a unique and creative sense of humor that we all loved and tried to emulate. I still love the memory of knowing that no matter how rough a morning we might have had on the set, I could count on an hour or so of laughing and blowing off steam with those two amazing women before heading back to a long, hard, sweaty afternoon. Rita, inspired by Yvonne, came up with the wonderful and hilarious thought of a Puerto Rican auditioning for *Gypsy*—"Curtain up, light the lights" all with a hysterically overblown and very "on purpose" Puerto Rican accent. That was the beginning of the character of Googie Gomez Rita created, which she performed on Broadway in *The Ritz*, for which she won a Tony.

The first time I saw Natalie Wood, she was walking up the alley to rehearsal. By herself. No entourage, no star behavior, even though she'd been acting in films since she was four years old. She was already a seasoned professional at the age of eight, when she had her first major role in the Christmas classic *A Miracle on 34th Street*. I heard someone say about her while we were filming *West Side Story*, "That's a camera face." Yes, it most certainly was.

Natalie was only twenty-three when we shot *West Side Story*, but she'd paid attention during her nineteen years in the business. She routinely invited several of us to her dressing room to relax, or play a game she loved, the specifics of which I've forgotten but it involved making choices. One day we were taking a break between scenes and talking about the fame, money, limos, the best tables at restaurants, just the privileged lifestyle in

Me and Yvonne Othon Wilder back at Goldwyn Studios, 1960

general that an acting career can bring with it. Natalie summed up the conversation with a wave of her hand indicating "all of it" with a simple, thoughtful, "This is all transitory."

Evidently Natalie never spoke to Richard Beymer off-camera, and he in turn didn't speak to her. They obviously had very important scenes together—he was, after all, the character of Tony/"Romeo" to Natalie's Maria/"Juliet." I always wondered why Bob Wise didn't say anything. Did he notice that they weren't speaking and try to help?

By the time Richard actually started filming, Jerry was gone, Bob said very little, and Natalie wasn't speaking to him. So he was alone!

I've heard that Natalie filmed to her own voice and that super "ghost singer" Marni Nixon laid in her own voice later. (Marni Nixon, by the way, wasn't contractually owed a percentage of the *West Side Story* soundtrack royalties, so Leonard Bernstein gave her a share of *his* royalties. She certainly deserved it, and how generous of him.)

Dubbed-in singing voice or not, I have always loved every moment of Natalie's performance as Maria. She had a unique gift of not just verbalizing and telegraphing every emotion her character was feeling but actually emanating them, as if she were lit from the inside. Whether you were in a scene with her or watching her from a seat in the theater, you didn't just know what her character felt, you *felt* what her character felt. I spent several casual evenings at Natalie's home after *West Side Story* wrapped, and she gave me another piece of advice I possibly should have taken: "Don't ever do a costume picture." But more about that later. . . .

As for Richard Beymer, I ran into him at the gym not that long ago. The subject of the film naturally came up, and he said, "You know, I could have tried talking to Natalie, I just didn't," as if he's spent all these years blaming himself for the offscreen distance between them. I assured him he has nothing to apologize for when it comes to *West Side Story*. He'd already made important films, like *The Diary of Anne Frank*, and *Indiscretion of an American Wife* with Montgomery Clift and Jennifer Jones, and *Hemingway's Adventures of a Young Man*, so he came to *West Side Story* very experienced. I thought he gave a wonderful, imaginative, soulful, non-stereotypical performance. A lot of people felt he'd been miscast as a reformed bad boy. I think there were times when *Richard* felt he'd been miscast, bolstered by the fact that his vocals were dubbed by singer Jimmy Bryant. But he took his portrayal of Tony very seriously, and he got no help from anyone on the film, not even from Robert Wise.

Don't get me wrong, Bob Wise was a brilliant man in so many ways, a man who, earlier in his career, when he was only twenty-four, edited Orson Welles's iconic *Citizen Kane*. Bob was extremely kind, and a true

Natalie in rehearsal

gentleman. But as a director, he wasn't always very communicative. One day between takes in the drugstore war council scene I went to Bob and said, "I feel like I could be doing more." He replied, "Yeah, you could." I waited for him to follow that up with, "Have you thought of . . . ?" or "You know, you might try. . . ." But no. Just, "Yeah, you could," the end. And before one of our dance scenes, Rita, who adored Bob, muttered to me, "If he says 'put a little salt and pepper in it' one more time, I'm going to scream." So I wasn't surprised to hear that Richard Beymer often felt so alone on the set that he'd go home from work and call his acting coach Sandy Meisner to ask for advice.

And as if Richard didn't already have enough to deal with, his first day in front of a camera was the day a shocking, emotionally disruptive bomb was dropped on the whole *West Side Story* production that none of us will ever forget.

But we still had a lot of filming to do before that day arrived.

One of the most ambitious and exciting numbers in *West Side Story* was the "America" sequence.

In the stage play, "America" was only performed by the girls. In the film, it was transformed to include the guys as well, which made it much more competitively playful between the guys and the girls while they sing about their different experiences as immigrants to this country. Some of the lyrics were changed from the stage to the screen version to soften the edginess of the theatrical production. Onstage, for example, the song begins, "Puerto Rico, you ugly island, island of tropic diseases. . . ." In the movie it's "Puerto Rico, my heart's devotion, let it sink back in the ocean." A few lines later, "And the babies crying, and the bullets flying" was revised to "And the sunlight streaming, and the natives steaming. . . ." In my opinion, none of these changes even slightly alter or affect the meaning and spirit of the number.

It took two and a half weeks to shoot "America," and I loved it. Not only was it fun, but I also felt it helped establish Bernardo's character. We had a little freedom to improvise in that number, too, when the girls watch while the guys play around and tease the girls. We got to invent the moves between us ourselves, and we all enjoyed the creative freedom of it. Apparently Jerry enjoyed it too—one day as we were leaving the studio, Jerry called out, "That was very good spirit today!" It was a memorable, well-timed shot in the arm from him.

I had another memorable moment with Jerry while we were rehearsing "America." Three of us guys had a variation during that number that included a double pirouette. Not a hard thing to do, but for some reason I couldn't find the traction I needed, and in rehearsals I was playing it safe and doing only one pirouette. Finally Jerry came up to me and quietly asked, "Are you only going to do one pirouette?" It wasn't a harsh criticism; it was simply a polite, respectful reminder, handled in a way that I appreciated so much. And of course when the cameras rolled, I was determined to give that man the best double pirouette he had ever seen! It was a small, relatively incidental question on Jerry's part, but it was also another one of those times Jerry didn't just encourage me, he inspired me.

Doing the double pirouette for Jerry Robbins in the "America" number, 1960

The "America" lyrics weren't the only changes in *West Side Story* when it made its way from the stage to the screen, by the way. United Artists and Columbia Records, who owned the rights to the soundtrack, had their censorship policies, and they weren't about to let those policies be violated. Looking back, some of those changes seem almost hilarious, considering what's perfectly acceptable in today's movies and music. But in the late 1950s and early 1960s, censorship was strict, carefully monitored, and non-negotiable.

On stage, for example, when Riff and Tony reaffirm their friendship, they pledge their loyalty to each other and the Jets "from sperm to worm." Apparently the word *sperm* was considered potentially offensive to public sensibilities, so onscreen and in the soundtrack that phrase was revised to "from birth to earth."

The Jets' "Gee, Officer Krupke" number was tidied up even more. The stage lyrics, "My father is a bastard, my ma's an S.O.B." became "My daddy beats my mommy, my mommy clobbers me" in the film. "Dear kindly social worker, they say go earn a buck, like be a soda jerker, which means like be a schmuck" was reinvented to, "Dear kindly social worker, they say go get a job, like be a soda jerker, which means I'd be a slob." And if the word *sperm* was unacceptable, imagine how quickly the censors put a stop to the stage ending of that song, "Gee, Officer Krupke—fuck you!" Sondheim cleaned that up to, "Gee, Officer Krupke—*krup* you!", which I happen to think was amazingly clever of him!

One of the most fantastic examples of the dancers' talent and Jerry's choreography in *West Side Story* was the "Cool" number with the Jets and their girls. Original, emotional, just extraordinary, and a real challenge to perform, with a lot of "knee work."

"Cool" is four minutes and thirty-nine seconds long in the film. Thanks to Jerry's perfectionism, it took three weeks to shoot it. Bob Wise was always there, of course, so it seems fair to assume that he was on board with Jerry's approach.

They shot the whole "Cool" sequence from the usual variety of angles. But rather than pick it up from certain starting points within the song,

Jerry insisted that the whole number be performed from beginning to end on every take. By the time they were finished filming it, the Jets had some nasty blisters on their knees, and they were so infuriated by Jerry's "beginning to end" demand that they piled their knee pads in front of his dressing room door and set them on fire.

Difficult as it obviously was, there's an intensity to that number in the film that would never have been there without Jerry. He wasn't being sadistic; he just knew what would elevate "Cool" from "good" to "great," and he knew how to make it happen. Carole D'Andrea, one of the girls in that number, said later, "It was worth every minute." And it was after "Cool" was finally in the can that I overheard two men from the front office talking in the alley outside the soundstage. One of them said to the other, "I think we might have an artistic success, but we're not at all sure we'll have a commercial one."

Apparently the executives were very happy with what we were doing; their only question was whether or not anyone would bother to buy tickets to watch it. Great. Then again, as writer William Goldman observed about the Powers That Be in show business in his book *Adventures in the Screen Trade*, when it comes right down to it, "Nobody knows anything."

It was a Sunday night, just over three months or so into filming. I was in my apartment, getting ready to fall into bed, when I got a call from assistant director Bob Relyea. The shooting schedule had been changed, he said, and we'd be moving on to the war council scene in the drugstore the next morning.

Fine with me. It wasn't the first time the schedule had been moved around so I didn't give it a second thought, let alone ask why.

I found out why the next morning, and I was devastated.

Chapter Six

IT WAS WHILE I WAS PREPARING FOR THE DRUGSTORE SCENE ON MONDAY morning that Russ Tamblyn gave me the news. The shooting schedule had been changed because on the previous Friday, two days earlier, Jerome Robbins had been fired.

Russ seemed happy about it, which I didn't understand at all. I just got very quiet, shocked and angry on Jerry's behalf.

Various Sharks and Jets with Jerry during a break in rehearsals. Back row: Jay Norman, Betty Walberg, me, Yvonne Othon Wilder, Tommy Abbott, Jerry, and Eddie Verso. Front row: Mrs. Norman, David Bean, and Tony Mordente.

How could this happen? Jerry was the most brilliant choreographer in the industry. He was co-directing the movie. It was Jerome Robbins who made this all happen! He conceived, directed, and choreographed both the Broadway production and the London production. None of that mattered? Okay, what about the fact that it was Jerome Robbins who sat down in his apartment one night in 1947 with Leonard Bernstein and Arthur Laurents and gave birth to *West Side Story* in the first place? That didn't count either? He was still expendable? Really?

From what I was told, Jerry's contract with United Artists and the Mirisch Brothers apparently specified that if, after three months, Jerry's involvement with the film wasn't working out, they had the option to let him go. I wasn't aware of it at the time, but it seems that filming was behind and over-budget, so much so that there were rumors floating around, rumors I hadn't heard, that we might not be able to complete the film. In the end, like it or not, there's a reason they call it show *business*.

There's no doubt about the fact that Jerry was exacting, a perfectionist, more with himself than with anyone else. Rita used to say, "It must kill him to hear the words 'cut and print,' because you know he wants to do it just one more time in case we could do it even better." But when she heard the news that he'd been fired, her reaction was, "Jerry was hard on us, but I would drop everything to work with him again."

Carol Lawrence, the original Maria on Broadway, has been quoted as saying of Jerry, "Everyone feared, dreaded and adored him."

One of the Jets, who'd obviously been part of the "do it on the other foot" episode during the prologue, asked rhetorically, "How do you fire God?"

Natalie loved what Jerry created for her so much, particularly the beautiful scene on the roof when Maria is daydreaming about Tony, that I heard she threatened to walk off the film if he wasn't rehired.

Walter Mirisch, who was burdened with the job of going to Jerry's house and firing him, described it as the hardest day of his long, storied career.

Jerry was so devastated by being fired that his first reaction was that he wanted his name taken off the picture. He never spoke to Walter Mirisch again and, in fact never made another movie. What a loss to the craft, and to the film industry. I'll never believe that *West Side Story* would have been the sensation it was without his direction, choreography, and presence.

Howard Jeffrey, out of loyalty, left *West Side Story* with Jerry. I would have done exactly the same thing if I'd been in his place. I admired Howard's loyalty to Jerry, what a blow it was, and how offensive this had to be to both of them.

Part of my anger on behalf of this extraordinary man was the fact that they had everything they needed from him. The only two sequences we hadn't shot yet were sequences that Jerry had already choreographed and rehearsed—the dance hall, and the rumble and the scenes with Natalie and Richard. They did not benefit from Jerry's direction in their scenes together. So now it was convenient to let him go. He had done the work.

When Tony and Maria met for the first time in the dance hall, Bob Wise did sixty takes. *Sixty.* And after the rumble, when Anybodys (Susie Oaks) came in to try to get Tony to leave, Bob did sixteen takes, without ever telling her why, or what was wrong with the takes they'd already done. But *Jerry* was arbitrary and took too long?

I was honored to be included in a tribute to Jerome Robbins at the Paley Center in 2018, on what would have been his one hundredth birthday. It was a much-appreciated opportunity to publicly offer *my* point of view, after years of experience with him. Not once did I personally hear Jerry Robbins raise his voice. Not once did he ever treat me with anything but decency and respect. Chita and I have talked about Jerry many times, and she had the same experience with him that I did.

I have nothing but the deepest respect for him.

Somehow, even though we were all reeling from the news that Jerome Robbins was gone, we made it through the drugstore scene on our first day without him . . . and Richard Beymer's first day on camera. That poor guy, what terrible timing, but he definitely rose to the occasion.

In Jerry's absence, Tony Mordente (Action) coached us through the dance at the gym and even worked in some gymnastics for Russ, if I'm remembering correctly. It made me smile that Irene Sharaff, in what I took as a subtle wink at me and the audience, dressed me for that sequence in a *shark*skin suit.

I can't think of that black suit and purple shirt without remembering one sunny day as I was walking alone down a street on the lot, headed to the set. Out of the blue, I suddenly felt the full force of the costume Irene had designed for Bernardo to wear for the dance at the gym. It was kind of a jolt, and even gave me a bit of a shiver. Her costume design helped me be Bernardo. It was proud, and it was elegant. It was Bernardo. It was also the first time I realized that just as Jerry Robbins choreographed for character, Irene Sharaff designed for character. She connected with their souls and expressed them through her mastery. No wonder she remains one of the most important designers in the history of stage and screen.

By the way, for all the pride and elegance I felt while wearing that suit, I still managed to split my pants twice during the dance at the gym. I changed into the only other pair they had for me, split those too, and ended up performing the whole number wearing black tights under my black pants to keep the censors from cutting the whole sequence.

It was a constant source of amazement to me how gracefully Robert Wise took charge after Jerry, his co-director, was fired. Bob had always been it seemed to me the "father figure" of the two, overseeing everything from the background, while Jerry was the one on the floor with us actors. It must have been a rough transition for Bob to take over on the floor, but he never let it show. He made it as seamless as possible for everyone and kept us moving forward, always efficient, always getting the job done. A perfect example was the scene in the drugstore when the Jets were mercilessly taunting Anita. Rita and the Jets rehearsed that scene and its choreography for about three hours, during which Rita had a meltdown, crying and unable to stop.

Rita related very closely to the character of Anita. She often said, "Anita *is* me," a proud, strong Hispanic woman with an iron-clad sense of self-respect. Rita was a child when her mother brought her from her native Puerto Rico to New York in search of a better life for her and her daughter. It was a source of deep pain and confusion to Rita that she immediately became the target of a lot of cruel teasing, rejection, and abuse for being a "spic." She couldn't imagine what she'd done wrong, and it shattered her self-worth. She fought hard to overcome it and thought she had overcome it. But during rehearsals for the drugstore scene, while the Jets surrounded Anita and brutally mocked her, Rita's memories and all that long-buried trauma came flooding back, and she broke. The Jets she was working with comforted her as best they could; she just could not stop sobbing.

Some directors would have been thoroughly exasperated and focused all their attention on how much time and money this delay in filming was costing. But Bob Wise focused all his attention on Rita. He called an early lunch and sat down with her to ask what was going on. He listened, and he cared; and in the end he encouraged her, not just for that scene but for life in general, to get tougher, to stand up to any cowards who tried to bully her, and to never let them win.

And sure enough, when the cameras rolled, Rita didn't just pull herself together, she soared. She left no doubt with her last line of the scene that she was a force for the Jets to reckon with, thanks to Bob's compassionately putting her back in touch with the powerful woman she is.

The Sharks and I present Bob Wise with a special cake during a rehearsal, 1960.

Decades after *West Side Story* I attended an evening devoted to honoring Robert Wise. After his many, many accomplishments were acknowledged, speaker after speaker took the stage to talk about him as an editor, as a director, and as a man. To be honest, after a while it almost got boring, for the best possible reason—there wasn't a single speech that didn't revolve around what an incredibly nice and decent man Bob Wise was, to the point where we started wondering if every speaker was tempted to simply step up to the mike and just say, "Ditto."

My ten-week leave of absence from Her Majesty's Theatre to film *West Side Story* finally ended eight months after it began. It was time to head back to London, back to the stage, back to playing Riff, back to my friends onstage and off, while leaving behind friends I'd come to treasure in the movie cast and crew. Shooting the film had been an unbelievable experience, but I was so happy to be performing Riff and the whole show in sequence again, no re-takes, no do-overs, no delays, and most of all, reconnecting with a live audience. I hadn't even realized until I was onstage again that first night how much I'd missed it.

In the meantime, of course, filming went on for another month before the long post-production process started, and buzz about the movie was starting to spread throughout the industry. It was exciting and nerve-wracking. There are few things less predictable than how an audience is going to react to a movie. All the hype in the world isn't going to keep theaters full if the film doesn't deliver, and I couldn't get the words "I'm just not sure we've got a commercial success" out of my head. There wasn't a doubt in my mind that *West Side Story* deserved to be a hit, and that all of us who were involved with it deserved to be proud of it. But this industry has a long history of "sure things" that audiences end up staying away from in droves.

I wasn't the only one who was going through waves of jitters as the movie's premiere approached. Rita found out people were going to be charged $5 apiece for tickets, and she was convinced that, at that price, we were going to be sitting by ourselves in an otherwise empty theater.

I actually didn't wait for the premiere to see the film on the big screen for the first time.

My friend Dru was working as a dancer on a TV variety show, *The Garry Moore Show*, and I did a guest spot on the show. One of the regulars on that show was a fiercely talented entertainer named Carol Burnett, who made everyone around her, including me, feel like an old friend.

The first time I saw *West Side Story* was at the Rivoli Theater in New York. I was with Dru and Carol Burnett, and we sat in the balcony. The audience seemed to love it. I, on the other hand, had a reaction I didn't see coming—essentially, no reaction at all. Maybe it was too overwhelming to watch it. Maybe I was too close to it. I don't know. But I honestly just sat there looking at it with no sense of connection to it, no clue that it was special to me, or even that I was in it. I really didn't get it. I was just glad people enjoyed it.

West Side Story, the movie, officially opened at the Rivoli Theater in New York on October 18, 1961, to an ecstatic sold-out house. And with only a handful of exceptions, the reviews were breathtaking:

Marquee for the opening of *West Side Story* at the Rivoli Theater in New York, 1960

"a magnificent show, a milestone in movie musicals, a box-office smash. It is so good that superlatives are superfluous . . . Natalie Wood sets herself firmly as the most important young star of the time . . . Russ Tamblyn and George Chakiris are sensational as the rival gang leaders . . . Rita Moreno is splendid. . . ." —*Hollywood Reporter*

"nothing short of a cinema masterpiece. . . . Perhaps the most striking aspect of it is the sweep and vitality of the dazzling Jerome Robbins dances . . . Natalie Wood is full of luster and charm . . . Rita Moreno is a spitfire as Miss Wood's faithful friend, and George Chakiris is proud and heroic as her sweetheart and leader of the rival gang." —*New York Times*

"a beautifully-mounted, impressive, emotion-ridden and violent musical which, in its stark approach to a raging social problem and realism of unfoldment, may set a pattern for future presentations. . . . Most colorful performance, perhaps, is offered by George Chakiris . . . Tamblyn socks over his portrayal . . . Rita Moreno, in love with Chakiris, presents a fiery characterization and also scores hugely." —*Variety*

With Rita Moreno at The Cocoanut Grove following the premier at Grauman's Chinese Theater in 1962

Film critic Pauline Kael wasn't nearly as enthusiastic, calling the dancing "a simpering, sickly romantic ballet," the dialogue "painfully old-fashioned and mawkish," Natalie Wood "so perfectly banal she destroys all thoughts of love" and the film itself "frenzied hokum."

But as always, moviegoers took a "we'll be the judge of that" position. The box-office numbers exceeded our wildest expectations; and as I write this, *West Side Story* remains the highest-grossing musical of all time.

The previews and opening nights around the world were thrilling. But nothing topped February 26, 1962, the night of the Royal Command Film Performance in the Presence of Her Majesty the Queen in Leicester Square. Russ, Richard Beymer, Bob Wise, and I rented tails in anticipation of being presented to the Queen, and we sat together during the movie. I only mention that to clear up one of those idiotic internet "facts"—despite rumors to the contrary, Richard did *not* get up and walk out in the middle of the film. He's never claimed that he was all that happy with his experience on *West Side Story*, but he sat right there with Russ and me through the whole thing, and he's too much of a gentleman to have done anything else.

By sheer coincidence, the Royal Command Film Performance took place on the same date as the announcement of the Oscar nominations in Los Angeles. We were all a little preoccupied with anticipation that night. We were afraid to hope, but it was impossible not to.

During intermission I headed to a bar in the theater. I'd only been there a few seconds when I glanced over and saw Bob Wise pushing his way through the crowd to get to me. He wasn't just smiling, he was beaming. I asked him what was going on.

He started with, "You're not going to believe this."

He was right. It was hard to believe, as "too good to be true" news often is.

Bob had talked to the West Coast. The Oscar nominations were in. Including eleven— *eleven*—nominations for *West Side Story*. Among them, Best Picture. Best Director. Best Supporting Actress—Rita Moreno. And Best Supporting Actor—me!

Meeting Queen Elizabeth at the Royal Command Performance of *West Side Story*, 1962

With Richard, Russ, and Leslie Caron at the Royal Command Performance of *West Side Story*

With Shirley MacLaine at the Golden
Globes, 1961

With Janet Leigh at the 1962
Golden Globes

It took days, a lot of handshakes and hugs and phone calls from my family and friends, and seeing it in print for it to even sink in: I was nominated for an Academy Award.

The 1962 Oscars were held on April 9 at the Santa Monica Civic Auditorium.

Rita and I went together. She'd just flown in from the Philippines, where she had a small role in what she described as "some crappy war movie." (If you don't want to know how Rita feels about something, don't ask her!) I'd just flown in from Hawaii, where I was filming the movie *Diamond Head* with Charlton Heston, Yvette Mimieux, and James Darren. But even the two worst cases of jet lag in jet lag history couldn't have dimmed our excitement that night.

Rita looked spectacular, in a gown she'd had made in Manila when the nominations were announced. We were hoping against hope that *West Side Story* would win for Best Picture, and we desperately wanted Best Director to go to Bob Wise and Jerry Robbins. As for how we felt about our chances of winning, neither of us had bothered to prepare an acceptance speech, and we didn't try to come up with them on the long

drive to Santa Monica. Instead, we devoted our driving time to practic-
ing our "loser faces," those frozen expressions where you show your teeth,
hoping it looks like an actual smile, because you know you might be on
camera, meant to communicate the improbable message, "I'm glad they
won instead of me."

It was so great to reunite with everyone in our "film family," all of us at
our most glamorous and looking forward to the evening no matter what
happened—it was an honor just to be there as nominees. I was especially
moved to reunite with Jerry on a happy night and see that fantastic smile
of his again, deserving to be at the Oscars to celebrate *West Side Story* far
more than any of the rest of us as far as I was concerned.

After a dizzying whirlwind of pre-ceremonies activities, from the red
carpet to photos to quick interviews to milling around saying hello to old
friends, acquaintances, and total strangers who seemed to know me so I
pretended to know them, it was finally time to take our seats. Bob Hope,
our host for the evening, took the stage, and the biggest night in show
business was underway.

I was relieved that the Best Supporting Actor category led off the
awards. I just wanted it over with. My heart was pounding, it was hard
to breathe, and I kept trying to remember all the "loser face" expressions
Rita and I had worked on. I barely even heard Bob Hope when he said,
"Here to present the award for Best Supporting Actor, please welcome
the lovely Shirley Jones."

Out onstage walked Shirley Jones, beautiful as always. I sat tight as
she read the list of nominees, almost feeling like that little boy in Tucson
again, in love with the movies, who'd somehow wandered into a room full
of superstars where he didn't belong.

"Montgomery Clift, for *Judgment at Nuremberg*. George Chakiris, for
West Side Story. Jackie Gleason, for *The Hustler*. Peter Falk, for *Pocketful of
Miracles*. George C. Scott, for *The Hustler*."

The only way I can describe my reaction to hearing her say, "And the
winner is . . . George Chakiris, for *West Side Story*" is that it triggered a
complete out-of-body experience. Many people have asked if I expected
to win. The answer is no. It's like buying a lottery ticket. You hope you'll
win, but you certainly don't expect to.

Apparently I made it from my seat onto the stage, took my statuette from Shirley and, hopelessly unprepared, came out with, "I don't think I'll try to talk too much, I just want to say thank you very, very much." Not the most memorable acceptance speech ever given, but at least I couldn't be accused of being too long-winded.

I was in such a complete daze that I only vaguely remember walking offstage, Oscar in hand, being led to the press room, and eventually, somehow, making my way back to my seat beside Rita. She was almost as out of breath as I was from what had just happened.

Oscar night, 1962

As if winning an Academy Award wasn't already more than I could begin to take in, I found out later that I was the youngest Best Supporting Actor winner in Oscar history at the time. I was so honored, and so humbled.

I was still "coming down" from that when Rock Hudson made his entrance onstage to present the award for Best Supporting Actress. He arrived at the microphone and proceeded to read off the list of nominees.

"Fay Bainter, for *The Children's Hour*. Judy Garland, for *Judgment at Nuremberg*. Lotte Lenya, for *The Roman Spring of Mrs. Stone*. Una Merkel, for *Summer and Smoke*. Rita Moreno, for *West Side Story*."

He opened the envelope during, "And the winner is...."

I could feel Rita next to me, bracing herself, waiting to hear the name Judy Garland, whom she was convinced was going to win.

So when Rock looked at the contents of the envelope and announced, "Rita Moreno, for *West Side Story*," she let out a completely genuine gasp of surprise before we hugged, ecstatic, and she ran up onstage. Rock Hudson handed her the Best Supporting Actress Oscar.

With nothing prepared, she managed a simple, "I can't believe it! Good Lord! I'll leave you with that," and Rock escorted her to the wings.

To this day, Rita's kicking herself about the brevity of her acceptance speech. I say it doesn't matter—what does matter is that that night, Rita Moreno, my co-star, my friend, became the first Hispanic woman to win an Academy Award. Enough said.

The awards rolled along beautifully, with one after another being presented to the *West Side Story* nominees. Best Sound—Fred Hynes and Gordon Sawyer. Best Art Direction—Victor Gangelin and Boris Leven. Best Film Editing—Thomas Stanford. Best Original Score—Saul Chaplin, Johnny Green, Irwin Kostal, and Sid Ramin. Best Costume Design— Irene Sharaff. Best Cinematography—Daniel Fapp. It was breathtaking to see our talented colleagues so deserving and surprised and ecstatic, triumphantly holding up their Oscars onstage, being applauded by a room full of the best in the business.

Then, out strode Bob Hope again, to announce, "And now, to present the Academy Award for Best Director, Rosalind Russell." Auntie Mame herself, the stunning Rosalind Russell, took the stage and read the list of nominees: J. Lee Thompson for *The Guns of Navarone*; Robert Rossen for *The Hustler*; Federico Fellini for *La Dolce Vita*; Stanley Kramer for *Judgment at Nuremberg*; and Robert Wise and Jerome Robbins for *West Side Story*.

The winners: Robert Wise and Jerome Robbins for *West Side Story*. Jerry was right up there onstage beside Bob Wise where he belonged, and as she handed him his Oscar, Rosalind Russell whispered to Jerry, "I told you."

Robert Wise and Jerome Robbins made history that night, receiving the Academy's first shared directing award.

Finally the time came for the last Oscar of the night. As always, for Best Picture. Presented by none other than one of my idols, the iconic Fred Astaire.

The nominees: *Tammy*, *The Hustler*, *Judgment at Nuremberg*, *The Guns of Navarone*, and *West Side Story*.

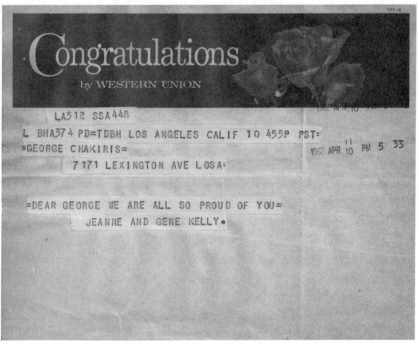

Telegram from Gene and Jean Kelly

The winner: *West Side Story.*

Robert Wise accepted, and during his speech he paid a special tribute to "those who created the original wonderful stage show—Jerry Robbins, Leonard Bernstein, Stephen Sondheim, and Arthur Laurents. All of us who had anything to do with putting *West Side Story* on the screen considered ourselves very fortunate to have had their wonderful material to work with."

"Very fortunate" doesn't begin to express it.

And with that Best Picture announcement, *West Side Story*, and the ten Oscars it received on April 9, 1962, became, and remains, the musical film with the most Academy Awards in history.

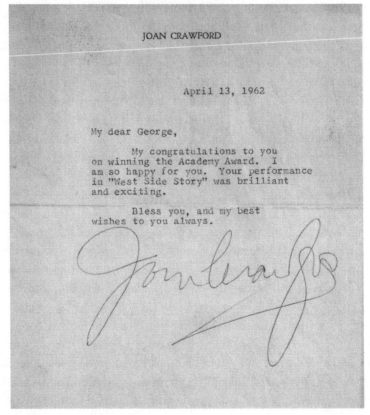

Letter from Joan Crawford

Chapter Seven

LIFE GETS VERY BUSY, NOISY, AND A LITTLE OVERWHELMING AFTER YOU win an Academy Award, maybe especially when you win an Academy Award in a movie that won Best Picture.

Suddenly I was inundated with agents and managers who wanted to sign me. Believe me, I was grateful, I just had no idea how to begin to sort out the offers that were coming in from producers and studios. This was my first experience in the "big leagues," and I was still incredibly naïve when it came to the business end of show business.

I also have to admit that I was a little bemused by my newfound popularity. Before *West Side Story* I'd somehow managed to get a meeting with a very highly regarded agent at the William Morris Agency. He couldn't have been nicer and more gracious . . . as he explained that they weren't signing any new clients at that time, but nice to meet you and best of luck. Now the William Morris Agency was among those who were waving contracts at me saying, "Sign here." As I'm writing this I'm suddenly remembering a childhood incident when my family and I were still living in Tucson. I was maybe ten years old, on an errand at our neighborhood grocery store, one of those homey little places with sawdust on the floor and proprietors who greeted everyone by name when they walked in the door. As I was leaving the store I looked down and, to my abject disbelief, I saw $9 cash lying on the floor. I quickly picked it up and raced home to show it to my mom, thinking it might help her pay for groceries or something. Instead of being pleasantly surprised, she made me go right back to the store and return the money. The money wasn't mine, it belonged to someone else, keeping it wasn't an option, end of discussion. I returned the money; and thanks to my mom, I learned that it actually felt good to do the right thing.

I'm blessed to have been raised by parents who lived with integrity and taught it to their children. I think some part of me assumed that everyone else was raised the same way, which obviously added to my naïveté and, in some cases, made me an easy mark to a handful of people who placed a higher value on "shrewdness" than they placed on character.

Of course, in the end, no excuses, I'm responsible for my own choices. Some of them have made me unbelievably happy, and some of them have cost me dearly.

In 1959, while I was playing Riff in London before *West Side Story* became a movie, I was approached by Saga Records, a small British label, to do an album of George Gershwin songs. My response may have been the quickest "yes!" in recording history. Who in their right mind would pass up a chance to record such classics as "Embraceable You," "I Got Rhythm," "My One and Only," "Someone to Watch Over Me," and "It Ain't Necessarily So"?

Saga had a collection of vinyl Gershwin orchestral tracks . . . ostensibly. They weren't good. In many cases it was even impossible to tell which songs were which. We had no choice but to start from scratch with a full orchestra.

Saga Records wasn't just a small label; it was a brand new label, full of enthusiasm and very low on money. I came in for the first day of recording and discovered that there was a slight problem—somehow someone at Saga had completely overlooked the fact that the orchestra had to be paid that morning or there would be no session. I couldn't let that happen, so I ran to the Midland Bank and managed to come up with just enough cash to bring back to the studio to pay the musicians for that session. Saga financially came through and the rest was smooth sailing.

We ended up with an album simply called *George Chakiris Sings George Gershwin*. I was and still am very proud of it. It got very nice reviews, including an especially flattering one from the esteemed British actor Richard Attenborough. I was playing the album on the record player in my dressing room one night before our *West Side Story* performance and Chita stopped in to make a sweet fuss over it. The whole experience was just incredibly satisfying.

It also taught me that I loved recording.

So I was blown away when, after that triumphant night at the Oscars, I got a call from Capitol Records. The *West Side Story* soundtrack had quickly soared to #1 on the *Billboard* charts (and, by the way, stayed at #1 for fifty-four consecutive weeks), and Capitol was offering me a recording contract. I signed it in the blink of an eye. They teamed me with some of their top-notch people, including Dave Cavanaugh, who'd just finished an album called *Sugar and Spice* with Peggy Lee (a favorite album of mine) and had produced for Nat King Cole as well. Dave and I did four albums together. It was thrilling.

And this is where a woman named Ruth Aarons enters the picture.

My friend Tony Hoover owns and operates a great company called Red Line Tours that gives tours of Hollywood and its history for students from all over the world. A few years ago I gave a talk to a group of fifty students from Scotland who were taking Tony's tour, and I gave them two pieces of advice: Pay attention to your instincts; and, with certain unavoidable exceptions, *never* sign over your power of attorney. I learned that second one the hard way.

I met Ruth Aarons through an agent named Jules Sharr at the William Morris Agency. She had a unique background. Her father Alex Aarons was a Broadway theatrical producer and co-creator of the Alvin Theatre in New York with his business partner Vinton Freedley. Her mother was an opera singer. After a wealthy, privileged childhood full of limos, a fully staffed house, and the finest schools in New York City, Ruth went on to become a world champion table tennis player. (Calling it Ping-Pong in Ruth's presence was strictly forbidden.) Next came a few years as a vaudeville performer, followed by establishing her own show business management firm.

In the wake of *West Side Story* and its massive global success, on the advice of my agent Jules Sharr, I became a Ruth Aarons client. Among the papers I signed with her firm was an agreement to give her power of attorney. I honestly didn't think a thing about it.

I'll be telling several Ruth Aarons stories throughout this book, not to indict her but to offer a cautionary tale for anyone who, like me, lets their naïveté prevent them from putting up boundaries, from saying no to assertive people with a need to control, and from taking charge of their own life.

One of the casualties of my professional relationship with Ruth was my treasured Capitol Records contract. I was having the best time, working with top-notch, talented, knowledgeable producers and arrangers, But for some inexplicable reason, Ruth didn't like them. She incessantly criticized them and complained about them to me. She never could give me an answer as to why she was so strongly opposed to them, which left me to guess that maybe it was because she hadn't chosen them, or maybe it was because they weren't especially interested in her creative input. A point came when I just learned to carefully avoid the subject of my recording career when she and I talked.

Then, one afternoon in the mid-1960s, three years into my Capitol deal, I was in my hotel room in Paris (more about that later) when Ruth called. It was a fun, light-hearted conversation. She brought me up to date on several things that were going on in my career, and we talked about Paris, which of course she loved, because who doesn't? We were ending the conversation when she tossed in, almost as an afterthought, "Oh, by the way, I've canceled your Capitol contract."

Click.

Recording session at Capitol Records, 1965

I was speechless. I was crushed. And I was livid, at her and at myself. Just like that, my recording career was over; and because I'd given her power of attorney, I didn't have a legal leg to stand on.

Maybe even more astonishing in retrospect—I didn't fire her. As more and more Ruth Aarons episodes unfolded over the years, friends kept asking me why I was still with her. The only answer I could ever come up with was that I thought I needed her. I'm sure my instincts screamed at me a hundred times to part ways with her professionally. But my insecurities about my ability to navigate the sometimes complicated, illogical, confusing world of show business kept overriding them. I did defy her a few times, and I never regretted it when I did. But overall, I stupidly ignored a lot of red flags. My mistake, not hers. It turns out Maya Angelou is exactly right: "When someone shows you who they are, believe them the first time."

The London production of *West Side Story* closed on June 10, 1961, after an amazing 1,040 performances. It was very hard to say goodbye.

Like almost every other actor on the planet, I was always wondering "what's next?" when a project came to an end.

Before I'd finished working on the *West Side Story* film, the Mirisch Company had signed me to a non-exclusive multi-picture deal. They saw the rushes at Panavision and decided I was potentially "hot," so it made sense for them, and they had nothing to lose—it was a "pay or play" contract, which meant I had to either show up or not get paid. I had no problem with that. For me it felt like a step up career-wise, and security in a way, and I was happy with it too. It probably would have been smart of me to hold off and wait to see what other opportunities came along. But I didn't think about taking jobs as part of a bigger, long-term game plan. I thought about them one at a time when offers presented themselves, and there was no help or guidance from my representation. I'd just signed with the William Morris Agency, and Ruth Aarons and I hadn't had the "long-term game plan" conversation; so while I waited for the Mirisch Company to cast me and start fulfilling our mutual commitment to each other, I simply got busy and appreciated how good it felt.

I'd shot a nice little black-and-white British movie called *Two and Two Make Six* while we were still onstage in London; and I'd committed to *Day of the Damned*, a Montgomery Clift film that never got off the ground.

I also got an offer from producer/director Roger Corman to do a motorcycle movie, *Wild Angels* with Nancy Sinatra and Peter Fonda. Even though the script wasn't finished yet, what I'd read sounded interesting, and I signed on to do it. Then the final pages of the script came in; and with no disrespect intended, it looked to me as if it was turning into a different kind of movie than I had been expecting. I wasn't comfortable with it and decided not to do it. Ruth was afraid Roger Corman would sue me; but he was very nice about it and let me out of my contract without a hassle, and he "struggled along" with Peter Fonda in my role instead. I've wondered more than once if it was *Wild Angels* that propelled Peter Fonda into making his classic film *Easy Rider*.

With Jackie Lane in *Two and Two Make Six*, at Elstree Studios London, 1960

Another film that I made during the busy year of
1962 was *Diamond Head* with Yvette Mimieux.

Then along came *Flight from Ashiya*, about an Air Force flight crew
on a mission to rescue survivors of a shipwreck during a typhoon. No
singing. No dancing. Just three lead actors, who, in the script, were doing
battle with their own demons as they embarked on this rescue mission, to
be shot entirely in Japan.

My co-stars were Yul Brynner and Richard Widmark. Suddenly,
thanks to the extraordinary success of *West Side Story* in Japan, the name
George Chakiris was appearing above the film's title beside the names
of two seasoned international stars. I remember getting off the plane on
the tarmac in Tokyo and finding police and security having to hold back
crowds of people who had gathered to see me and call out to me as I was
hurried along to the press room. All pretty overwhelming for a guy who's
never been comfortable being the center of attention, but it was so kind
of them, and I couldn't have imagined a more appreciative welcome for
my first trip to Japan.

Head shot from *Flight from Ashiya,* 1961

Yul and Richard were at opposite ends of the personality spectrum, which was fascinating to watch offscreen. They were both perfectly nice and very professional. Other than that, they couldn't have been more different.

Richard was a quiet, private, serious man who didn't seem interested in unnecessary attention. He arrived in Japan alone. His wife Jean joined him later, although we never met her or saw her. My friend Nan Morris came to spend time with me during filming, and nothing gave her more pleasure than trying to make Richard smile. She worked hard at it, and he did smile, reluctantly, a couple of times.

Nan and I were having dinner one night with the film crew at a local restaurant. Our tables were at the large front picture window. I saw a cab pull to a stop at the curb, with Richard in the back seat. Richard looked

Arrival in Tokyo, 1961

The traditional
Japanese green
tea ceremony,
Tokyo, 1961

out, saw all of us sitting inside, and had the cab pull away. We didn't take it personally. After spending day after day with us, it was perfectly understandable that he wasn't interested in hanging out with us at night as well.

Richard and I spent a lot of time on a huge soundstage in the Toho Studios in Tokyo, sitting next to each other in a mock-up of a helicopter cockpit with the control panel in front of us. Richard, being the good, responsible, professional actor he was, made himself very familiar with the controls so he could use them properly in the scene. I'm embarrassed to say that I didn't do that. I was a little too preoccupied with the script pages I'd put on the floor for reference, just in case.

After a few takes, with me sometimes glancing down at the pages at my feet and probably ignoring the control panel, Richard suddenly stopped a take, turned to me and yelled, in a very loud voice that reached every corner of the soundstage, "Why don't you read the script?!"

Everything and everyone came to an abrupt halt, and so did I. I didn't know what to say, what to do or where to look. I was mortified. After a very brief pause, I had to get up. I couldn't sit in that cockpit for another second. I walked away from the set into the dark studio. Our director, Michael Anderson, came over to calm me, and I managed to say, "I can't work with him!"

Yes, I actually said that. About Richard Widmark. Even I can't believe it.

It took a while, but of course I managed to calm down and compose myself, and of course I went right on working with him, especially after I realized that he was absolutely right. What on earth was I thinking? As a theater performer, I always checked my props before every show. How did I manage to completely overlook them here, in a scene with an actor I admired so much? It was not normal behavior for me. I'm a responsible person, but this one escaped me.

I could only come up with two possible explanations. One was that this was my very first time getting equal star billing above the title in a major film with Yul Brynner and Richard Widmark, no less. It was an actor's dream come true, and when it happened to me, I didn't know how to comfortably handle it. The responsibility of it—and it is a responsibility—hadn't dawned on me. The other was that maybe the responsibility *had* dawned on me, and it scared me. To this day I don't know.

With Yul Brynner in *Flight from Ashiya*, 1961

With Richard Widmark in *Flight from Ashiya*

Working in *Flight from Ashiya* in Japan, 1961

But Richard had done exactly the right thing by calling me out on my lack of focus. He took it upon himself to say what needed to be said when no one else was doing it. He was such a decent man, and over time I could sense that he was sorry he'd said it so harshly. The message was clear—he brought professionalism to every scene, and he expected it in return, from me and of course from everyone else, as it turned out.

And then there was Yul Brynner. He arrived with an entourage that included his sweet, beautiful Japanese mistress "Silky"; his secretary; his son Rocky; and his personal assistant, an elegant class-act Scot named Walter Lees, who was a war hero and intimate friend of everyone from the Duke and Duchess of Windsor to dancer Margot Fonteyn to shipping magnate Stavros Niarchos, and, thanks to *Flight from Ashiya*, me. Yul was a star, and he lived like one. He liked attention as much as Richard didn't, and there was no such thing as being in a room or a restaurant or on a soundstage with him without his making sure you knew he was there.

Quiet as he was, as I'd learned firsthand, there was a toughness about Richard that made it clear he was not to be messed with. Because there were essentially three storylines in the film—Richard's, Yul's, and mine— there would be days in the rushes when one of us didn't appear. When that "one-of-us" turned out to be Yul, he wanted rewrites so that he'd have more screen time. Richard wasn't having it, and it never happened. I admit I admired him for it, too. He did the right thing and took on Yul Brynner and won. I would never have dreamed of doing that and would not have known how to do such a thing.

Flight from Ashiya finally wrapped. It wouldn't be the last time I saw Tokyo, or even Yul Brynner, for that matter. But for now, the Mirisch Company had decided they were "ready for my closeup," and I was joyfully off to Pinewood Studios outside of London to shoot a movie for them called *633 Squadron*.

633 Squadron was a pleasure from beginning to end. Reasonable people coming together to work on a good movie, and not a tantrum in sight.

I played Lt. Erik Bergman, a Norwegian resistance fighter who guides the Royal Air Force to a German rocket fuel factory in Norway.

Cliff Robertson played Wing Commander Roy Grant, a pilot with the RAF Mosquito Force, whose mission is to take out the German factory.

With Cliff Robertson and Maria Perschy in *633 Squadron*, 1963

Maria Perschy played my sister Hilde, Grant's love interest.

Cliff Robertson was as easy, gracious, and congenial an actor as I'd ever worked with. Not an ounce of ego in him. A true gentleman who was good to everyone on the set. He also happened to be a certified pilot who'd served in the Merchant Marine in World War II. He loved World War II aircraft and was already the proud owner of a British Spitfire and other fighter planes as well. *633 Squadron* used authentic Mosquitoes, British twin-engine combat aircraft, in the film, and he was seriously considering buying one. He was a man of many interests and just fascinating to be around. He was an exceptional, ethical man.

Maria Perschy was a darling girl, comfortable, accessible, and totally devoid of pretense. She was very beautiful, with blonde hair and blue eyes. I, of course, had brown hair and brown eyes, and we played siblings; but we decided that if I could pass for Norwegian, Maria and I could certainly pass for brother and sister. She taught me how to make a great salad dressing using the sugar, mustard, and olive oil that was on every table in the Pinewood Studios commissary.

Our director, Walter Grauman, was very accomplished and as unaf-flicted by ego as the rest of us. He also spent four years in the Army Air Forces flying combat missions over Europe, which I'm sure significantly contributed to the fact that the flying sequences in *633 Squadron* are still considered some of the best ever filmed.

To add to the sheer fun of shooting *633 Squadron*, Ruth Aarons hadn't unceremoniously canceled my contract with Capitol Records yet, and I was still filming when the time came to record my second album for them.

As Oscar winners the previous year, Rita and I were presenters at the 1963 Academy Awards.

My producer Dave Cavanaugh and his team flew to England to make it happen. We recorded at Abbey Road Studios, one of the world's most acclaimed recording studios, made famous by the Beatles—they recorded there many times, and the cover of their classic *Abbey Road* album, with the four of them walking single file across the actual Abbey Road, was taken very near the studio. Their very esteemed producer George Martin worked with us, completing a great team and a great time. Some of my acting friends from *633 Squadron* even came to sit in on some of the recording sessions.

The end result was the album *You're Mine, You*, a collection of beautiful standards like "As Time Goes By," "The Best Is Yet to Come," and "Our Day Will Come," orchestrated with very soft Latin rhythms.

A fantastic memento of yet another wonderful, productive time in London.

Presenting the Oscar to Patty Duke, 1963

My next project for the Mirisch Company turned out to be another film with Yul Brynner, *Kings of the Sun*. Now, instead of playing a Norwegian as I had in *633 Squadron*, I was playing a Mayan prince, and Yul was playing a Native American. As we headed off to our location in Mazatlán, I couldn't get Natalie Wood's words out of my head: "Don't do a costume picture."

There was only one hotel in Mazatlán in those days, and we all stayed there—except Yul and his wife Doris, who joined him on this shoot. The production provided Yul and Doris with a house. Yul also had a trailer on location with walls of palm fronds placed around it for privacy, and he routinely had chili flown in from Chasen's, one of the most famous celebrity hangouts in Beverly Hills. Yul never left any doubt that he knew exactly who he was and what he was doing. He had that magnificent speaking voice, that uncompromising, unapologetic masculinity, and a self-assured awareness that he was a bona fide sex symbol.

In costume for *Kings of the Sun*, 1963

Yul's role in *Kings of the Sun* required him to be nude from the waist up. He happened to be naturally pale, very white, and it took a lot of makeup to transform him into a Native American. But once the transformation was complete, Yul Brynner was the King again, assuming an almost exaggerated version of that iconic *The King and I* walk that kind of amused everyone on the set. There was a shot of him and "his people" walking toward the camera; and at the end of the take Yul's friend and castmate Brad Dexter, who was standing beside me off-camera, called out, "Show them where the money is, Yul." No one could ever accuse him of failing to do that.

I never went to the rushes on that film, but Yul's wife did. I always had some idea of how I was doing depending on how warmly, or not, Doris treated me. While I never got to know her well, she seemed to be what I came to think of as kind of a friendly snob, one of those perfectly pleasant people who leapt at every possible opportunity to work names like "the Duke and Duchess" or "Liz and Dick" into a conversation whether or not they had anything to do with what we were talking about.

Our director on *Kings of the Sun*, J. Lee Thompson, was a nice man, and God knows he had his hands full on that film, but I found him a little less than inspiring. My character, a Mayan prince named Balam, was opposed to human sacrifice. Lee told me one day between takes that he thought we were doing an anti-capital punishment film. I thought he was reading a bit much into the script, but okay, whatever.

I had a fairly tough speech at the end of the movie, and I knew I really needed to deliver. The good guys had prevailed, and Yul's character had died, bravely and profoundly, of course. It was up to Balam (me) to speak to hundreds of "my people" from atop a pyramid and reassure them that all was well. The first line of the speech was, "Hunan Cel [the villain in the film] is dead." It was important, written to deeply move Balam's people (and hopefully the audience), and mine to deliver.

I'll never forget Lee's deeply thoughtful and inspiring direction moments before my cue: "Think of Laurence Olivier."

Gee, Lee, thanks a lot. That's a real help.

If anyone in *Kings of the Sun* was the poster child for Natalie's warning, "Don't do a costume picture," it had to be the wonderful, distinguished actor Richard Basehart, who played a Mayan priest. I don't know what sadistic idiot designed his look for that movie, but he emerged from hair and makeup every day looking like my grandmother. Or, as a *New York Times* critic observed, "[Basehart] looks [in this film] like the late Maria Ouspenskaya." He was too nice and too much of a pro to speak up about it, but it was really outrageous, and I'll always wonder how the people in charge allowed that to happen.

The female lead of *Kings of the Sun* was a darling, funny English actress named Shirley Anne Field, a natural redhead with stunning blue eyes. Dark makeup, a black wig, and voilà, she was Mayan. As long as it gave me the opportunity to work with her, why not?

Shirley Anne became one of my heroes while making that film. There was a bright, charming local boy who was one of the many extras on that film. We all fell in love with him and tried unsuccessfully to figure out how to help get him an education in the States. Shirley Anne in particular took him under her wing. She went out of her way to meet his mother, who spoke no English and whose husband had long since abandoned her and their son. They lived in hopeless poverty, in a shack with dirt floors, corrugated tin walls, and an oppressive smell. This little boy had never seen a toilet until Shirley Anne invited him and his mother to her hotel room. I've wondered many times what happened to that boy who was noticed and adored by everyone. God bless him and his mother, and most certainly Shirley Anne Field. What a kind, caring woman, and what a pleasure to have worked with her.

When *Kings of the Sun* finally wrapped, we all boarded a chartered Mexicana Airways four-engine propeller plane to head home—Yul, Doris, Shirley Anne, Richard Basehart, Brad Dexter, Lee Thompson, me, and as many others as the plane could accommodate. The first stop en route to Mexico City from Mazatlán was Guadalajara, about an hour away. It was one of the longest hours of my life.

Anyone who's ever flown has experienced turbulence. It's unpleasant, no one likes it, you're glad when it's over with, and in the end, oh, well. But as I learned on that flight, there's turbulence, and then there's the *turbulence* we went through on our way to Guadalajara—severe, relentless turbulence, compounded by steep banking by the pilot, sudden changes in altitude, more steep banking, lurching and violently bouncing in midair, way too far off the ground for comfort. . . . Just when I thought I couldn't get more terrified, I glanced over at Yul and saw that *he* was scared. Yul Brynner, scared. Let us pray.

By some miracle, we landed in one piece in Guadalajara, and I literally kissed the ground when we deplaned. After a brief layover it was time to reboard to continue on to Mexico City. I couldn't do it. There wasn't enough money or a big enough gun to get me back on that plane. Everyone else gamely got on board, and they reached Mexico City after what they later described as another turbulent hour. I reached that same destination eight hours later in a taxi. Believe me, it was worth the extra eight hours to stay right there on the ground and be alive to move on to anything but another costume picture.

Chapter Eight

AFTER A FEW MORE MOVIE OFFERS, SOME OF WHICH HAPPENED AND some of which didn't, I was off to Italy to play a costume-free Greek terrorist in *McGuire, Go Home!* The leads were Dirk Bogarde, Susan Strasberg, and Denholm Elliott. Count me in.

The enormous respect I'd always had for Dirk Bogarde only grew as we made that movie. He was a quiet, reserved, no-nonsense man who'd served in the British army during World War II. There was a palpable substance about him—it was immediately apparent that he had no use for shallow Hollywood glitz and posturing.

Before we started filming, Dirk invited us to his home, Nore Farm, in Surrey, in the south of England. Beautiful as it was, the thing I remember most about his house was that there was only one photograph in the whole place. It was on his piano, a framed picture of Ava Gardner, his costar in the movie *The Angel Wore Red*. I thought what a remarkable woman she must be to have earned an honor like that from a man whose respect was handed out so judiciously.

We shot part of *McGuire, Go Home!* in the gorgeous landscapes of Foggia, Italy, southeast of Rome. It was a pleasure for the most part. There was only one misstep, and it was so idiotic that even I had to speak up about it.

As I mentioned, I was playing a terrorist named Haghios who was working for the Greek resistance in Cyprus. High up in the chain of command. Powerful. Ruthless. Menacing. Striking fear in the hearts of anyone and everyone who got in his way.

Some of my scenes involved my character driving a convertible. On the day we were shooting those scenes, I was presented with my convertible. Not just any convertible—an older model Ford convertible. But wait, there's more. It was *pink*. Let's see. A dangerous, highly ranked Greek terrorist, roaring around Cyprus in an old pink Ford convertible. In a Mel Brooks movie? Hilarious. In *McGuire, Go Home!*? I don't think so. In fact, *no!*

To my profound relief, the producer and director agreed with me. We didn't shoot scenes with me in my car that day, or any other day, until a driver arrived from Rome with the perfect car—a *red* Ferrari convertible. Now, that felt exactly right. It was only to be driven by me when it was necessary for a scene, which was understandable, since the first Ferrari they sent was involved in an accident on the way to our location.

I loved that red Ferrari convertible, and I loved the driver they sent to teach me how to drive it. He was a real pro, and I can still hear him instructing me to accelerate only *prima et dopo curva* [before and after curves]. Trust me, I followed his orders to the letter. The thought of being responsible for a second Ferrari crash on that movie was enough to keep me awake nights.

Me in the red Ferrari from *Maguire, Go Home*

I'll always be grateful that I had the opportunity to work with Dirk Bogarde. If it hadn't already been apparent that he was a genuinely good man, his close friend Olga Horstig-Primuz, who also happened to be my agent in Paris, thought the world of him. Olga's eyesight was failing. Knowing that, Dirk wrote his letters to her in big, bold print. Even then she would struggle sometimes. She once asked me to read one of his letters aloud to her. I was flattered that she would trust me with something so personal, and the beautiful, heartfelt letter of friendship he wrote to her made me admire him even more.

Olga was very special herself, smart, sweet, and fiercely loyal to her friends and clients. Her apartment in Paris doubled as her office, and it showed. It wasn't furnished to impress, it was furnished to be used. When you stepped through the front door you were facing a hallway, at the end of which, on an easel, sat a magnificent picture of Olga's treasured client Brigitte Bardot.

With Susan Strasberg and Dirk Bogarde during a break in filming *Maguire, Go Home*, 1965

Still from *Maguire, Go Home*

Olga invited me to join her and Brigitte one night at the Westwood premiere of Brigitte's latest movie, a Louis Malle film called *Viva Maria*. I met them in their suite at the Beverly Hills Hotel. Brigitte was running a little late, so Olga and I had a few minutes to catch up before Bardot emerged from the bedroom and made her entrance into the living room. Good God, she was stunning. That long, gorgeous hair, that spectacular body in a soft orange gown, a wonderfully warm smile . . . and almost as irresistible as her looks was the fact that she was completely unpretentious. Both at the hotel and in the limo on our way to the premiere, the conversation was easy, comfortable, and fun; she was happy to talk about any number of subjects other than herself, and she spoke perfect English.

As Vincent in *The Theft of The Mona Lisa*, 1964

Hordes of press, cameras, and fans were lining the red carpet when we arrived at the theater, all of them breathlessly waiting to see Brigitte Bardot. She was no novice at this. She knew exactly what and who her public wanted, and she gave it to them. It was fascinating to watch that sweet, down-to-earth woman I'd just been chatting and laughing with in the back of the limo transform herself into a glamorous international sex symbol/movie star for the several minutes it took us to get from the curb to the theater entrance through the crowds, photographers, and microphones.

There was a reception and dinner after the screening, and I sat with Brigitte at our table there. I enjoyed almost studying how at ease she was with everyone who stopped by to say hello to her, including Paul Newman, and have their picture taken with her. Without a trace of phoniness, she treated each of them, whether they were a celebrity or a "civilian," as if she was genuinely happy to see them and they mattered to her. It's a rare social gift, one I've always wished I wasn't too introverted to master as well as Brigitte.

But I was, and I am, as evidenced by what happened after the reception. Brigitte wanted to go dancing, and I was too shy to accommodate her. In my defense, I've never been a social dancer, and I couldn't imagine how disappointed she'd be if I tried to lead her around a dance floor. She was great about it, but still. . . .

In case you're keeping score, my shyness had now kept me from dancing with Elizabeth Taylor and Brigitte Bardot. I shake my head over it to this day. But between the fact that she was one of the most stunning and gracious women I've ever met, and she also happens to be a world-renowned animal lover, I'm a Brigitte Bardot fan for life.

By now I was renting a charming guest house at the end of a pretty little tree-lined cul-de-sac off of Benedict Canyon in Beverly Hills. The guest house and the main house, which I eventually moved into, were owned by a talent manager named Rudi Altobelli. One of his clients, Henry Fonda, had preceded me in the guest house. Henry Fonda was a talented artist, and a painting he'd been working on was still there on an easel.

With Shirley Jones, 1965

With Ann-Margaret, about 1965

It was in that house that I got a visit from writer/director Jacques Demy and composer Michel Legrand, who wanted to talk to me about a French musical film they were getting ready to do called *Les Demoiselles de Rochefort* (*The Young Girls of Rochefort*). They told me the storyline of the movie, and they brought a recording of the music, vocals and all.

I loved everything about it, including the names attached. The French cast started with the exquisite Catherine Deneuve and her real-life sister Françoise Dorléac (Dorléac is the family name), playing twins who are dreaming of love and new lives in the world outside of their home town of Rochefort. The "foreigners" in the film were going to be Gene Kelly, me, and the talented dancer/choreographer Grover Dale (who, incidentally, played Snowboy in the original Broadway cast of *West Side Story*). We Americans would have our dialogue and songs dubbed in French.

I had seen and loved Jacques Demy's *The Umbrellas of Cherbourg*, also starring Catherine Deneuve, and I was a really big fan of Michel Legrand's music. I was excited about *The Young Girls of Rochefort*.

The William Morris Agency wasn't. Neither was Ruth Aarons.

"George, it's an ensemble film!" she said when I told her about it, as if it was the dumbest idea she'd ever heard. "Who would want to do an ensemble film?"

The answer was, I would. And I did. It was one of those times when I ignored her advice and her dismissiveness, and I never regretted it.

The press, always compelled to categorize people and draw comparisons, commonly referred to Catherine Deneuve as the "cool" beauty and her sister Françoise as the "warm" beauty. I take a firm "whatever" position on that kind of thing. Take it from someone who saw them without makeup many, many times—you couldn't have taken a bad photograph of either of them if you tried. What made them even more attractive was how funny they were, and how adorable they were with each other. They were loving, playful, always there for each other, without a hint of the sibling rivalry that could easily have existed between two gorgeous sisters in the same business and in the same movie.

With Francoise Dorleac during the filming of *The Young Girls of Rochefort*, 1966

With Catherine Deneuve in *The Young Girls of Rochefort*, 1967

In France, the director is the real star of any film, and Jacques Demy, who was also the writer of *The Young Girls of Rochefort*, was no exception. Incredibly gifted? No doubt about it. Knew how to make absolutely stunning movies? Yes! What I didn't know until we arrived on location was that he also had quite a temper.

To be fair, I'm sure this film was a big deal for him. It was a French-American Warner Brothers film, his chance to become an international director, rather than "just" a French director. His previous film, *The Umbrellas of Cherbourg*, had been a huge success, was nominated for several Oscars, and won three awards at the Cannes Film Festival. But still, it was a "French film." The plan for *The Young Girls of Rochefort* was to release both a French version and an English version, which meant we had to get good, solid takes in both languages.

I met up with Catherine Deneuve again in Paris in 1978.

Rochefort was further challenged by the fact that it included major dance sequences—not just any dance sequences, but dance sequences featuring Gene Kelly. Our choreographer, Norman Maen, was meeting those challenges beautifully; but Gene, with his background and experience in musical film, understandably wanted to be involved in creating his musical numbers.

Kelly's way of creating musical numbers was very different from Demy's. Jacques was obviously a very gifted director/editor, but he didn't want to decide what piece of film he would use for a sequence until he saw it on film. Nothing wrong with that, but it did mean excessively long takes so that he had a lot of film to choose from.

Gene, on the other hand, knew before he ever stepped onto a set exactly what he wanted to see onscreen. Each section of a number was created, choreographed, and rehearsed to be seen from a particular angle. His camera work was original and superb. With Gene at the helm, the camera moved as well. It was alive. It was part of the scene. And it was efficient. As far as Gene was concerned, pre-designed camera moves were as important as the steps or vocal phrases when it came to creating a musical number, so that the angle for each section was all you had to photograph. Why waste time and energy shooting a section of a number that isn't constructed to be seen? In other words, Gene's brilliantly organized approach to shooting musical numbers was pretty much the polar opposite of Demy's long takes/shoot-it-all-and-figure-it-out-in-the-editing-room approach.

To Demy's credit, he did respectfully edit a ten-minute musical sequence and screen it for Gene and a few of the rest of us at a local theater. It was outstanding, although Gene was unhappy with the way he looked and yelled at his image on film, "Get off the screen!"

The one time I saw Gene genuinely happy during that shoot started with a letter to me from his wife Jeanne Coyne. In the letter she told me that Gene's birthday was coming up on August 23. She couldn't be there to celebrate with him, but she still wanted to surprise him with his

Jacques Perrin, me, Catherine Deneuve, Danielle Darrieux, Francoise Dorleac, Michel Piccoli, Grover Dale, Gene Kelly, 1967

The Young Girls of Rochefort dinner scene with Grover Dale, me, Danielle Darrieux, Francoise Dorleac, and Catherine Deneuve, 1967

favorite breakfast—eggs, toast, corned beef hash, and a great cup of coffee. She knew I'd never be able to find corned beef hash in Rochefort, so she sent some, along with a personal card from her to Gene.

Grover Dale and I got the hotel chef to prepare this special off-menu order; and on August 23, room service presented Gene with his favorite breakfast, the note from Jeanne and a single long-stemmed red rose. At first he thought maybe she'd come to Rochefort to surprise him, and he was a little disappointed to learn that she hadn't; but that breakfast, her thoughtfulness, and the trouble she'd gone to to make it happen on his birthday gave him such pleasure. He loved it so much, and I loved doing it for both of them.

Jacques had taken on a real challenge with *The Young Girls of Rochefort*, no doubt about it, and pressure does tend to amplify the rougher edges of people's personalities.

The first bump in the road between Jacques and me started with what I thought wasn't a very big deal. All the male dancers in the film, including Grover and me, were dressed in exactly the same trousers and boots, with different colored shirts for different scenes. Apparently the "who wants to do an ensemble film?" argument had somehow worked its insidious way into my subconscious; and I asked if maybe Grover and I could wear trousers of a slightly different color, to set us apart from the rest of the dancers. I actually ended up asking twice, with no response. I got the feeling the second time that Jacques was getting annoyed with me, so I didn't mention it again.

I wanted to clear the air between us before we started shooting, and I called him to apologize for asking in the first place and make sure he knew how genuinely happy I was to be there.

His response was to simply snap back, "I don't care if you come naked!"

Okay. Got it. Tread lightly. And I did . . . but I also pressed my luck one more time.

There was a "kermesse" (carnival) sequence in the film that took over the entire square of Rochefort. Countless extras, booths everywhere, and Grover and I had a booth because we were in charge of the whole thing. We were wearing very spiffy bright white motorcycle gear, and I was maneuvering a big, heavy stationary Harley Davidson on a swivel. In case you've ever wondered, it turns out that even on a swivel, Harley Davidsons don't want to be spun. Our great choreographer Norman Maen kept trying to come up with interesting swiveling moves on that bike, to very little avail. But Jacques had told me when we first met that he was going to "do his best" to create a number just for me, and I thought maybe this was it . . . except that Grover's and my spiffy white motorcycle outfits were accessorized by spiffy white motorcycle helmets. And what better way to make yourself unrecognizable than to put on a motorcycle helmet?

I didn't understand. I'd become recognizable by the time we shot *The Young Girls of Rochefort*, and if that could contribute to a little more business at the box office, why not take advantage of it?

"Jacques," I pointed out, reasonably, I thought, "if I'm wearing that helmet, no one will know it's me."

Nothing.

So I kept spinning and trying to think of some way to get rid of that helmet. Next I came up with, "You know, Jacques, the helmet covers my ears, and I can't hear the playback."

He was immediately responsive to that—he had them drill ear holes on both sides of the helmet, which obviously didn't make me any more recognizable, since I doubt if I could pick my own ears out of a lineup.

Finally I decided that maybe we could bridge the communication gap if I simply asked for an explanation.

"But Jacques, why do I have to wear this helmet?"

He answered at the top of his lungs, in front of the other dancers, the multitude of extras in the Rochefort square, and the large French crew, with an explanation that didn't require a translator:

"Because you're a ****!" (Think of the most vile word you know. It's not in my vocabulary. I can't even bring myself to write it.)

I was mortified to my core. And it didn't endear Jacques to anyone within earshot, either. Between that outburst and the relentless, exhausting Harley spinning, the minute we finished filming the sequence, I raced to the nearest toilet and threw up. So much for that number created just for me.

I was almost relieved to discover that it wasn't just me who triggered Demy's explosive side. The production itself managed to push him over the edge too.

We did a lot of filming outdoors on the square, and obviously you need fairly consistent decent weather to film exteriors. The production had built a real coffee house on the square, where the fabulous Danielle Darrieux filmed most of her scenes as the mother of the two girls. (It was a great coffee house, incidentally, that served real beer, real coffee, and the best *pomme frites* I've ever eaten.) So when the weather turned bad, the production asked Jacques to move inside to the café. Then weather suddenly cleared up, and they asked him to move back outside. Then more bad weather, back inside, good weather again, back outside . . . it went on and on. Any director would have found it frustrating. But it became too much for Jacques, and he decided to sulk. He leaned back on the fountain in the middle of the square, told his assistant director to take over, directed the rest of the sequence by proxy, and refused to speak to anyone.

The minute each of us was finished with our work on the film, we practically ran to board the train back to Paris. Catherine left Rochefort a few days after I did, and we had drinks together at the Raphael Hotel when she arrived, just to decompress. It seems Jacques had even made *her* cry. They'd done *The Umbrellas of Cherbourg* together a few years earlier, and she said she'd never seen him behave this way.

I believe that. There's no doubt about what a beautifully talented man he was. I also don't doubt that he was, in his heart, a nice man under a lot of pressure, with a passionate commitment to *The Young Girls of Rochefort* that showed on the screen. Expletives, vomit, motorcycle helmets, ear holes and all, that "ensemble film" has become one of the favorite films of my career.

Filming in Italy was always an adventure. The 1960s were very successful for Italian movies, both financially and artistically, and I was lucky enough to be offered several of them. In contrast to shooting in America, though, there was always a more relaxed atmosphere in Italy that made perfect sense to me. Lunch wasn't just a break, it was something to be lingered over and appreciated with a glass of wine. Food was important.

All of which added to my excitement when I was cast in one of my favorite projects, a film called *La ragazza di Bube* (*Bebo's Girl*). It starred Claudia Cardinale and was directed by Luigi Comencini. Its producer was Franco Cristaldi, a man whose work I greatly admired and who would go on to win an Oscar for his classic film *Cinema Paradiso*. I loved Claudia Cardinale, a stunning, gracious young woman and a very talented actress who was a pleasure to work with. The screenplay was based on a popular Italian true story about a young girl (Claudia) who falls in love with a Communist partisan (me) in the wake of World War II. It was a serious film, and I've sometimes thought that Cristaldi, Claudia's mentor and future husband, intended *La ragazza di Bube* to be for her what *Two Women* was for Sophia Loren. I was proud to be part of it and part of Italian cinema in the great decade that included directors such as Luchino Visconti, Vittorio De Sica, Federico Fellini, and of course Luigi Comencini.

With Claudia Cardinale in *Bebo's Girl*, 1964

Publicity shot with Claudia from *Bebo's Girl*

But along came what had to be my last day of work. I had a firm stop date, which is a contractual date when the production was obligated to finish with my scenes for the film and let me go.

We finished shooting at our location in the Italian countryside of Siena and drove, right on time, to what would be my final location on the film. And by "we," it turned out, I mean "everyone but the camera crew." Somehow, somewhere, they seemed to have vanished between locations.

Impossible, but true. There we all were, ready to shoot but nothing to shoot *with*, nearing nervous breakdowns because in just a few more hours, I had no choice, I was out of there. The sun wouldn't be out much longer, there were no real roads in the countryside, there were certainly no cellphones in those days, or any other way to reach the camera crew, to find out where they were and why, and guide them to where we were all waiting. And waiting. And waiting. While frustration was building. And building. And building.

I have no idea how long we sat there: the director, the producer, and the rest of the production team getting angrier by the second. But finally the camera crew and equipment made their leisurely entrance, and the yelling and screaming began. It was all in Italian, of course, but I didn't have to be fluent to know that whatever they were shrieking at each other, it was definitely *not* "Are you guys okay?" and "Sorry we're late." I'd never seen such rage and so many out-of-control temper tantrums in my life . . . for about ten or fifteen minutes.

Then, just like that, it was over. Out of their systems, done, everything was fine, they were all pals again, ready to go back to work as if nothing had happened. It was jaw-dropping. None of them seemed to give this confrontation a second thought, while my stomach churned about it for days. I actually kind of envied it. For all the over-the-top drama and name-calling, it was probably healthier and more productive than brooding and holding grudges. Maybe even more amazing, though, was that after all those hours of waiting for our wandering camera crew and the confrontations that followed, we finished filming right on time, and my contractual stop date was faithfully honored.

By the time I did another American co-production in Italy, I'd learned not to take that leisurely approach to filmmaking too seriously. In fact, I enjoyed it.

The film was *The Theft of the Mona Lisa*, a remake of a 1931 German film. The timing of our first day of shooting there was unfortunate. Rome and the surrounding areas had been flooded with torrential rains. Trains were off their tracks. Lorries were overturned. The houses in the poverty-stricken lowlands were filled with mud and debris. Newspapers reported that the Pope would be visiting the disaster victims a few days later to give them his blessing. The angry victims were quoted as saying, "We don't need your blessing! We need money!" I couldn't honestly say I blamed them.

Our hearts went out to those people, and all that tragic chaos made it much easier to keep the filming glitches and holdups in perspective. Complaining that some props weren't where they were supposed to be, or the camera crew was late, seemed too petty to even warrant a passing comment, especially on a film I really enjoyed making. It was an opportunity to have a role that wasn't overly serious, a role that I could have fun with, and I was ready for that.

In front of the George V Theatre on the Champs Elysees where *West Side Story* had been playing for five years

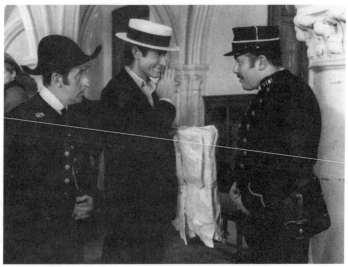

The *Theft of the Mona Lisa* (wrapped and under my arm), 1966

"Caper" movies were making waves in the 1960s, thanks in large part to films like *How to Steal a Million* with Audrey Hepburn and Peter O'Toole, the Rat Pack's *Ocean's 11*, and *The Thomas Crown Affair* with Steve McQueen and Faye Dunaway. They had intentionally over-the-top plots that were part of the fun of making them and watching them.

The Theft of the Mona Lisa was no exception. It was a period piece, based on the true story of a worker at the Louvre in Paris, Vincenzio Perugia, who hid in the museum one night after it closed and, on August 21, 1911, casually walked out with Leonardo da Vinci's masterpiece wrapped in his white smock and tucked under his arm. No one noticed until the following day that the painting was gone. (During this time it was even thought that Picasso might have stolen the painting.) The Mona Lisa was finally returned to the Louvre twenty-eight months later, in January of 1914.

I played Vincent, the professional thief in the film, sporting a straw bowler hat and early 1900s clothes. I also had to smoke strong cigars that made me ill but looked good and helped my character. I'm okay with getting ill as long as it looks good.

My character's plan to steal the painting in *The Theft of the Mona Lisa* is very deliberate and intricate, and he methodically achieves his goal. In the story, near the Louvre is the Mona Lisa Hotel, where all the young women on duty are made to look and dress like the Mona Lisa. One especially beautiful girl looks so much like the Mona Lisa that she captures Vincent's heart and imagination. He has to meet her. He has to know her. He pursues her, of course, and a romance follows, as well as a chase from other thieves who want to steal the painting from him. It all leads to a happy ending, roll credits.

The girl in the film was played by a glorious, stunning, talented French/Russian actress named Marina Vlady, who'd recently won the Best Actress award at the Cannes Film Festival. It's worth looking at *The Theft of the Mona Lisa* just to see her.

Our French director, Michel Deville, was actually the reason I wanted to do the film in the first place. My agent Olga Horstig had highly recommended him, and with good reason. He was well respected, he knew how to make beautiful, charming, elegant movies, and he also understood the fun and the spirit of *The Theft of the Mona Lisa*. What a pleasure it was to get to work with him.

Another highlight of making that movie was hanging out with Dascha Auerbach, the daughter of our American producer. She was a delight. She introduced me to bellinis (champagne with peach nectar), and she shared a joke that gave me a much-needed laugh while we were working our way through filming in Italy:

"What's the difference between German hell, French hell, and Italian hell?

"In German hell you get wine, women, song, amazing food and drink, steins of beer, pretzels, anything you want for twelve hours. For the next twelve hours you are living in fire and brimstone, being beaten, tortured, starved to death, and nailed to the cross.

"In French hell you get wine, women, song, champagne and caviar, escargot, anything you want for twelve hours. For the next twelve hours you are living in fire and brimstone, being beaten, tortured, starved to death, and nailed to the cross.

"In Italian hell you get wine, women, song, a free pass to the Vatican, spaghetti, lasagna, very dry Italian white wine, anything you want for twelve hours. For the next twelve hours you are living in fire and brimstone, being beaten, tortured, starved to death, and nailed to the cross . . . but sometimes they forget the hammer and nails."

So maybe we should have seen it coming that once the film was in the can, our Italian producer, who'd never produced a movie before, decided to take the film out of Michel's hands and edit the film himself. He managed to make the story almost incomprehensible, and even lost some of the footage in the process, which is even worse than forgetting the hammer and nails. Our American producer tried with some success over the years to retrieve the film and recover some of the missing footage, and somehow he managed to restore it. In spite of the Italian producer's well-intentioned meddling, *The Theft of the Mona Lisa* remains a beautifully photographed, and very enchanting movie. I loved working on it.

As a perfect period at the end of filming, by the way, we spent a few days on location in Paris, and the entire team went to the George

V Theater on the Champs-Élysées to see *West Side Story*, which was still playing there after five years. What a great way to wrap a great shoot.

I didn't want to leave Paris. No one ever wants to leave Paris. But I had some packing and moving to take care of back in L.A.

The lease was up on the Rudi Altobelli house I was renting off of Benedict Canyon. I'd lived in the two-thousand-square-foot guest house for a year, and then in the thirty-two-hundred-square-foot main house for another year. I'd loved it there. It was quiet and just secluded enough, very French Country, on three acres, with a pool, lots of pine and cherry trees, and a private driveway. I knew I'd miss it, but it was way more space than I needed, and I had too much traveling ahead to justify staying there anyway.

Sadly, I'd see that house again, a few years later, on the news. So would the rest of the world.

Chapter Nine

In early 1968 I was invited to the Acapulco Film Festival. I'd never been to Acapulco before, and I'd always heard how beautiful it was, so of course, thank you, I'd love to.

I was booked on a nonstop flight from Los Angeles to Acapulco. I'd just settled in to the first-class cabin when my seatmate boarded the plane—a young, very pretty Mia Farrow, en route to the same film festival.

It took almost no time at all to discover that Mia also happened to be very nice, very intelligent, and very talkative. It was great fun to find myself seated next to her. She had just finished a Joseph Losey film, *Secret Ceremony* with Elizabeth Taylor, and I was always interested in hearing Elizabeth Taylor stories from sources as reliable as the one who was suddenly sitting next to me.

Mia said she couldn't help but notice that despite the fact that Elizabeth arrived quietly on the set every morning for the day's shoot, no fanfare, no diva behavior, the crew, the other actors, *everyone* was so in awe of her that they found it hard to treat her as just another actress in the movie. Part of it was her iconic beauty. Part of it was her reputation. (By then, Elizabeth's scandalous marriage to Eddie Fisher had ended and she'd fallen madly in love with and married Richard Burton.) And part of it was simply that she was Elizabeth Taylor.

Even the director Joseph Losey seemed to be a bit in awe of Elizabeth. She knew acting on film inside out. She'd appeared in her first film when she was ten years old and starred in *National Velvet* when she was twelve. She was known for never doing more than two takes of a scene, and Joseph Losey never asked her to do more. Mia told me, with nothing but respect, that she thought Elizabeth's performance could have been even better if Losey hadn't been too intimidated to ask for more takes if necessary.

Farrow also emphasized that none of this—the awe, the intimidation, the deference from everyone on the set—had anything to do with Elizabeth's behavior. She never made the cliché demands of a star. She never condescended to anyone, as stars have certainly been known to do. She never acted like a star. She just *was* one, and she seemed to be the only person involved in the production who was unaffected by it. I loved hearing that.

Mia was a perfect traveling companion. As much as I was looking forward to Acapulco, I was a little sorry when our plane landed and the flight and our conversation were over. After deplaning we were driven to the Las Brisas Hotel, where the festival guests were being accommodated. Mia didn't want to stay there. If I remember correctly, she was still married to Frank Sinatra at the time and went off to stay at his home instead. But thank you again, Mia, for our really enjoyable four hours together.

The 1968 Acapulco Film Festival became infamous for the riot that broke out over the controversial Mexican film *Fando y Lis* that was ultimately banned in Mexico. My experience, though, was an evening of spectacular people at their spectacular best, there to have a good time and celebrate their latest projects.

In retrospect, one of my more memorable moments that night was running into Sharon Tate and her husband Roman Polanski. She was sweet as could be, and stunning in a sparkly minidress and thigh-high boots. There was a lot of excitement around her and Roman, thanks to her latest film *Valley of the Dolls* and Roman's recently released *Rosemary's Baby*, starring my new pal Mia Farrow; and it was fun watching Sharon handle all that attention with such unentitled grace.

I actually got to spend an evening with her many months later at her and Roman's beach house. Roman was away somewhere. She was a sweet and darling hostess to the few of us who were gathered there, and she invited us to spend the night, which we did. Read nothing into that; it was purely innocent, simply a kind gesture to spare us the drive from the ocean all the way back to my place at some ungodly hour.

Bonnie and Clyde won the Best Picture award at the Acapulco Film Festival that year. Warren Beatty wasn't able to attend and I'd been asked to accept the award on his behalf. It was a handsome statuette, about eight inches high, a sculpted gold-plated head on an ebony-colored base. Unfortunately, after the ceremony, I hadn't been told who to give it to. I asked everyone, and no one seemed to know or care, so in the end, I reluctantly held onto it. I felt a little odd running around with a Best Picture award for a movie that I had absolutely nothing to do with, but I swear, I tried hard to find a more appropriate recipient.

It so happened that Darryl Zanuck's daughter Darrylin was living in Acapulco at the time. She held a fundraiser called DAR every year, a charity she founded to benefit several local orphanages. Her father was the president of 20th Century Fox, and Darrylin screened his films at these fundraisers and flew in actors like Kirk Douglas, Rock Hudson, and Paul Newman to enhance the publicity and the donations.

She went out of her way to introduce herself to me at the awards ceremony, while I stood there with my shiny new *Bonnie and Clyde* statuette, and invited me to attend her upcoming benefit. As if I needed more incentive to say yes, she added that she was screening *A Flea in Her Ear* with Rex Harrison and Rosemary Harris, whom I'd happily find myself working with years later. And by the way, if I'd accept Darrilyn's invitation, I was welcome to stay in Acapulco as her guest for as long as I liked.

She didn't need to twist my arm. I loved everything about Acapulco, particularly the weather. I've always enjoyed spending time in the sun, and for whatever reason, maybe the moisture in the air, the weather there made it possible to spend hour after hour in the sun without getting burned. I would never do this now, but in 1968, when none of us knew any better, everyone worked on their tans. I spent every day for the next two weeks working on mine. I got incredibly dark, which I thought looked fantastic. Finally, reluctantly, I decided it was time to get back to L.A., after a wonderful, relaxing, unexpected vacation. I was almost literally walking in the door with my luggage when Ruth Aarons called to ask me to come to a party she was giving that night for Dionne Warwick's husband Bill Elliott. Like everyone else on the planet, I loved Dionne, and her husband seemed like a good guy. Jet-lagged or not, I wanted to see Dionne, and

Ruth always threw great parties, so I pulled myself together and drove to Ruth's house.

I ended up being the target of a lot of good-natured laughter and kidding that night. Most of the guests were Black; but with the exception of Dionne, thanks to the Acapulco sun, I was the darkest guest at the party. It wasn't remotely racist; everyone thought it was just fun and funny and a memory that still makes me smile.

As luck would have it, I was back in Acapulco again in what seemed like the blink of an eye, to shoot *The Big Cube*. I'd turned it down a couple of times because of some problems with the script; but once those were taken care of, I said yes. Only then did they mention that the star of the film was going to be the original "Sweater Girl" herself, Lana Turner. I'd come this close to passing up a chance to work with Lana Turner? I'd still be kicking myself.

I've never forgotten the first time I saw her. I was on the MGM lot filming *Brigadoon* with Gene Kelly, and there she was, alone, walking by on her way to the set. She was shooting a movie called *The Prodigal*, in which she played a Damascus love goddess, and she was in her pagan priestess wardrobe that day. Just breathtaking, with the most secure, straight-backed, confident walk I've ever seen. I remember thinking that it would have been impossible for any other actress to fill those stilettos, and wondering how hard it must have been for the crew to stop gaping at her long enough to get anything done. The legend of Lana Turner being discovered buying a Coke at the Top Hat Cafe on Sunset Boulevard when she was sixteen years old? One look at her and there wasn't a doubt in my mind that it was true.

So it was kind of a fantasy-come-true to suddenly be co-starring with her, playing a womanizing medical student in *The Big Cube*, with Richard Egan and Dan O'Herlihy. I have no idea what I was expecting, but it certainly wasn't the gregarious, down-to-earth breath of fresh air she turned out to be, a real professional who never needed more than two takes per scene and who insisted we all call her Lanita. I'll always believe that it's mostly because of Lana Turner that *The Big Cube* is now a popular cult film.

Testing LSD in *The Big Cube*, 1969

Trying to harm Lana Turner in *The Big Cube*, 1969

I'd just returned to my hotel room one night after a day of shooting when my sister Athena called. She had a hard time getting the words out, but finally she managed to break the news to me: Our father had suddenly had a stroke, and just as suddenly he was gone.

If you've been through a moment like that, you'll understand why I can't find the words to describe it. The pain is so sudden, so deep, and so profound that you can't begin to take it in all at once. And sudden or not, the loss of a close loved one is an ache that never quite goes away. There's no way to prepare yourself for the waves of that ache that keep hitting you as time goes by and you realize that they're really gone, and they're really not coming back.

I flew home first thing the next morning and spent five days with my mom and siblings, holding each other up through our grief and making arrangements to lay my precious dad to rest.

It was a huge and loving tribute with family and many friends who all adored my father.

Once *The Big Cube* had wrapped and I was back in L.A. for good, it was time to go house-hunting. Dad had passed away at home, and my mom, my younger brother, and my sister, who'd been living there with him, were understandably finding it too hard to stay there with those memories.

We looked at a lot of houses until Mom fell in love with a great one near Mulholland Drive in the Hollywood Hills with four bedrooms and a pool. I bought it and moved into it with my mother and two siblings. I was busy working, making good money but not around much, and it made me feel good to be able to take care of them.

While all that was going on, there had also been a personnel change or two among "my people." My agent Jules Sharr had moved into the public appearance department of the agency and his wife Ina Bernstein, a former ABC casting director who'd joined IFA, had become my TV, film, and theatrical agent—not a great arrangement as far as Ruth Aarons was concerned.

Ruth had a brother named Lisle. They were incredibly close, so inseparable that they lived in the same apartment building on 47th Street in New York and went into business together when Ruth formed her personal management firm. Ruth handled the "artistic" side, and Lisle handled her clients' finances.

Then Lisle passed away, still in his forties; we were all really worried about how in the world she would handle his being gone. She eventually "replaced" her brother as best she could with Jules Sharr. Ruth and Jules became very close, and she was very possessive about Jules, me, and everyone else she thought of as "hers"; so she regarded Ina as an intruder.

Ina and Jules had an interesting history together. She was in love with him when she developed a serious physical problem, something that caused her stomach to get hard and extremely distended. Her doctor recommended surgery. She was justifiably terrified and asked Jules if he would marry her if she survived. He said yes, he would. She survived, and they married. Happily they did really well as a couple.

Ruth, on hearing the news that Ina's surgery was successful, imagined, to Jules and me, Ina's surgeon announcing, "Congratulations, it's a nine-pound tumor." Her sense of humor was dark sometimes, but she could be very funny and make me laugh, even when, like that time, it might not have been in the best taste.

Thanks to Jules, now in charge of my public appearances, I was booked into my first Las Vegas engagement at Caesars Palace. It was perfect timing, exactly what I needed after losing Dad, and I was excited and ready to take it on.

My Vegas show was designed for me, two other guys, and two girls. I didn't have any of my own songs on the hit parade, but I had an endless supply of cover songs to choose from that I loved and loved to sing, like "The Impossible Dream." Ruth hired her friend Jonathan Lucas to stage the show, and he did a wonderful job with the opening number. It was smart, it was well crafted, and it came together in no time at all.

Unfortunately, Jonathan, talented as he was, didn't really have much of an answer to the question, "And then what?" For the next couple of weeks we kind of struggled along with one number after another that were okay at best. I was getting very worried, imagining opening onstage in Las Vegas for the first time in my life to an audience that was yawning their way through the show and wondering how much longer they had to sit there. I finally sat down with Julie and Ruth one night after yet another "okay" rehearsal to figure out what to do.

Ruth's advice was abrupt and impulsive and caught me completely off guard: "I think we should cancel."

Not a chance. I wasn't looking for a way out, I was looking for a way to keep things moving. We found one in director/producer/choreographer Paul Gleason, who took over and turned things around. Jonathan Lucas was terrific about it, not offended, and he stayed on and kept right on working with us. I really appreciated him for that.

Caesars Palace billboard in Las Vegas, 1968

Caesars Palace show, 1969

Opening night exceeded all our expectations. It was a lot of fun, it was energized, the packed house amplified our excitement onstage, and the reviews were spectacular. The only person who wasn't excited about it was Ruth. She arrived with an attitude, sullen and resentful, and she didn't drop it all evening. I don't think she smiled once. My assumption, knowing her as well as I did by then, was that she wasn't about to enjoy a show that went on against her advice and without her control. I noticed, and I didn't appreciate it; but I refused to let her distract me with a guilt trip on an otherwise perfect night.

We all have aspects of our lives we would love to go back and do differently. One of mine is how carelessly I handled my involvement with Ruth over way too many years.

Of course there were times when I thought of letting her go, but I could always come up with plenty of reasons not to, beyond my standard "I thought I needed her." Ruth could be an absolute delight. She was a fantastic cook and knew how to throw a great party. She had other clients I knew and respected—Shirley Jones, Jack Cassidy, David Cassidy, Susan Dey, Celeste Holm, and Janis Paige, to name a few—and if she was good enough for them, she must be good enough for me. She came from a prestigious theatrical family, which logically implied that she had a lot more show business savvy than I did. We all went to her doctor, Dr. Milton Uhley. And because I've never been good with money, when Ruth recommended I sign on with Lee Bush, the business manager she'd hired when Lisle passed away, to handle my finances and investments, I didn't hesitate, let alone ask questions—if I'd have even known what questions to ask.

I had been in the house off Mulholland for just a few years when Ruth and Lee told me I couldn't afford to keep it anymore. I needed to sell it, they said.

It didn't feel right or make sense to me. I'd been working nonstop and making perfectly good money but Ruth and Lee were the "experts." So I ignored my instinct that this was the wrong thing to do and sold the house.

"Where did all the money go?" is one of the most commonly asked questions in the entertainment industry. I can't speak for anyone else, I can only look back and say for myself that, in the end, I ignored my instinct that something was wrong, something didn't add up. I didn't ask the right questions and demand answers I could understand. I didn't seek out another professional for a second opinion. I just went on with my career and assumed that because I had a personal manager and a business manager, I was covered by "experts" in areas I wasn't gifted at. My fault, not theirs. I let it happen.

Learn from my mistakes. Do better than I did, stay vigilant and listen to your instincts. Trust me, it will be a lot more peaceful than asking yourself years later, over and over again, "What on earth was I thinking?"

Ruth and I still had a long way to go before finally parting ways.

Chapter Ten

IN 1969 I FINALLY RETURNED TO THE STAGE FOR THE FIRST TIME SINCE *West Side Story*. I'd almost forgotten how much I loved the theater. It was more wonderful to be back than I could ever have imagined.

The Corn Is Green is a beautiful play by Welsh writer Emlyn Williams. We performed it at the prestigious Ivanhoe Theater in Chicago, under the direction of George Keathley. The icing on the cake was my co-star Eileen Herlie, a Scottish-American actress with an enviable resume that included her role as Sir Laurence Olivier's mother in his film production of *Hamlet*. She was such a strong, gifted professional that she was completely convincing as Olivier's mother, despite the fact that in reality, she was only eleven years older than he was.

Ivanhoe Theater in Chicago for *The Corn is Green*, 1969

Eileen played Miss Moffatt in *The Corn Is Green*, a middle-aged schoolteacher who comes to a small Welsh mining village to help educate the young men in the mines, over the strong objections of the local squire. She gives them the assignment of writing an essay; and as she reads the essays she discovers that one of her new students, Morgan Evans (me), shows a rough artistry that impresses her. She focuses her efforts on him, thinking she can possibly save him from a future of nothing but backbreaking work, borderline poverty, and probable alcoholism by helping him win a scholarship to Oxford. After some moving plot twists that involve attempted blackmail, a young woman, and a baby, Morgan does win the scholarship, and Miss Moffatt convinces him not to pass up this opportunity to make the most of his gifts, create a worthwhile future for himself, and contribute something to the world. I loved this play and what it had to say. *The Corn Is Green* is a life-affirming, semi-autobiographical work that was produced on Broadway starring Ethel Barrymore and made into a movie starring Bette Davis.

To make absolutely sure I did my character justice, I studied with a local Welsh minister to perfect that musical, lyrical accent and fell in love with it. I was determined not to let myself down after too many years away from the theater. I was even more determined not to disappoint Eileen Herlie. Most of my scenes were with her, and she'd worked with the best of the best, from Olivier to Dirk Bogarde to James Mason to Montgomery Clift. She was a generous, powerful performer. I wanted her to think the same of me.

So wouldn't you know, on opening night, in our final, climactic scene, I dried. Which means I got lost. I couldn't begin to find my lines, or think of what on earth I was supposed to say next. It's every stage actor's nightmare, and it's terrifying. But Eileen, with her rock-solid composure and expertise, rescued me. She caught right on to what was happening with me and started asking questions in keeping with the basic content of the scene, without ever breaking character—so patient, so focused, and so smart that she managed to guide me back on track without the audience ever catching on that the scene wasn't proceeding exactly as written. She saved me, she saved the play, and she earned my eternal respect and gratitude in the process. From that night on, I never went onstage for that scene without reviewing the lines one more time, and I never dried again.

All of us involved in *The Corn Is Green* shared the unique, fascinating experience of frequently performing matinees for audiences of young people who averaged about twelve to fourteen years of age.

The first time it happened, we were completely disoriented by the response of our new young audience. They laughed in places we'd never heard laughter before. They cried in places we never saw coming. We were scratching our heads backstage, trying to figure out what was going on and what we were doing wrong, especially when it kept happening, matinee after matinee.

In time, we realized we weren't doing anything wrong at all, nor were our young audiences. They were with us 100 percent; they just brought their own refreshingly open, untainted perspective. It didn't even occur to them to censor themselves, and their responses were exquisitely honest. Before long we found ourselves looking forward to performing for them.

With Eileen Herlie and some young audience members after the performance of *The Corn is Green*, Chicago, 1969

We figured out that their unexpected responses weren't criticisms; they were actually approval, confirmations that we'd established a connection with them. We went from confused to honored, and we also learned a sweet lesson about the value of honesty.

The Corn Is Green at the Ivanhoe Theater was a huge success. The run was extended for several weeks. And for me, it was all serendipitous—a great play, a great theater, a great director, and a great co-star, a perfect blend of elements for my return to the stage after so many years.

Perhaps even more than that, though, on a purely personal level, it restored my confidence as an actor. I didn't choose some of my film roles carefully enough after *West Side Story*, or even knew that I could. Some of those roles I would happily choose again. Others I wouldn't. I was so focused on what I thought was the film's potential box office success; or on an actor or director or producer I wanted to work with; or on a location that sounded like a great place to visit that I didn't pay nearly enough attention to what my part in it might require of me. Would it challenge

Publicity photo shoot at Goldwyn Studios, 1969

me? Would it stretch me as an actor? Was it a role I could really sink my teeth into? Would it be a smart choice for building a long-term career? If not, why didn't I just say no and be more patient and selective?

But thanks to *The Corn Is Green*, I got to *act* again. I loved it, I needed it, and I'm so thankful to Eileen Herlie, to George Keathley, and to Emlyn Williams for the opportunity to re-light my fire. One of my treasures from that collaboration are two personal letters from Emlyn Williams. I had such admiration for him and his writing.

I was back in L.A. by late summer. On August 9, 1969, I was visiting my friend and wardrobe mistress Charlotte Starbird, hanging out in her living room, casually chatting, with the TV on but muted. We noticed "breaking news" and live shots of a fleet of cop cars parked on a residential street with their lights flashing, but with no sound we didn't really pay much attention.

Then they showed a helicopter shot of the house where all those cop cars had gathered. It was the Rudi Altobelli house, the house and guest house where I'd spent two happy years: 10050 Cielo Drive. Obviously something terrible had happened there. It wasn't until we turned on the sound that the unbelievable horror hit me.

Sometime during the night, the occupants of that property had been slaughtered: that darling Sharon Tate and her unborn baby; her friends Abigail Folger and Wojciech Frykowski; Steven Parent, there just to visit the caretaker who was living in the guest house; and my friend and hair-dresser Jay Sebring.

It was beyond words how outraged I was, how outraged the whole city was.

I thought that if there had been a posse, whoever committed this atrocity would already be dead. And I might have joined that posse. . . .

I thought of Roman Polanski, in Europe making a movie, and couldn't imagine what it must have been like for him to be so far away and get the news that his wife and baby had been so viciously killed.

I thought of all the other friends of Sharon and Roman's, and clients of Jay's, who could easily have been there that night and randomly murdered, apparently without a moment's thought—Warren Beatty, Jack

Nicholson, Steve McQueen, Kirk Douglas, Sharon's sister Debra, and so many others.

I thought of the other people who, like me, had lived at 10050 Cielo Drive over the years—Henry Fonda, Cary Grant and Dyan Cannon, Olivia Hussey—and imagined that they must be as haunted as I was by being able to picture the horror much too clearly.

Just thinking about it all these years later still brings up those same feelings—the outrage, the tears, the hollow, unimaginable senselessness, inside the walls of that exquisite house where it seemed as if nothing bad could ever happen. Those poor, innocent victims, who had no way of knowing when they woke up that morning that they wouldn't live to see another sunrise . . . reminding me from time to time that none of us knows what might happen or how much time we might have left on this earth, so we owe it to ourselves, and to those we love, to make the most of every moment we've got.

Some time after the horror on Cielo Drive, I mustered up the courage to finally visit Rudi Altobelli, who'd cleaned up the house and the grounds and moved back in with a couple of guard dogs. It was eerie and uncomfortable. I didn't stay long, and I never went back again. I've been told that Rudi finally sold the property, the structures there were demolished and replaced by a 12,000-square-foot mansion, and the street address has been changed to discourage the nonstop stream of trespassers, tour buses, and curiosity seekers. Some part of me likes knowing that nothing that was there in August of 1969 is there anymore, not even a single brick or stick of wood or blade of grass.

I happened upon another "Sharon Tate house" connection a few years later, completely by accident.

It started in Athens, Greece. I was sitting with a few friends in a virtually empty coffee house when a lovely stranger came over to our table and extended her hand to me.

"Forgive me," she said, "I don't think you know me, but my name is Nana Mouskouri, and I'm doing a musical TV show in Paris. I would love it if you would be my guest."

It was such a modest, respectful introduction. I gave her my phone number in London, where I was headed in a few days. I soon learned that Nana Mouskouri was a popular Greek singer—in fact, one of the most internationally successful singers of all time. The gentleman who was with her turned out to be the prolific Greek composer and lyricist Mikis Theodorakis. Ms. Mouskouri kept impressive company. So did Mr. Theodorakis.

Nana did call me in London, and I had a fantastic time doing her show in Paris, with the added bonus of being choreographed by Norman Maen, our choreographer on *The Young Girls of Rochefort*. Nana became a good friend and convinced me to stay in Paris to do several more shows with her, which led to my own special for French TV and recording for Polydor Records.

I ended up spending a lot of time in Paris and getting to know some fascinating people there—Omar Sharif, Alain Delon, Jean-Paul

With Nana Mouskouri in Paris, 1975

Belmondo, the breathtaking Sophia Loren, and renowned director Sergio Leone, creator of the "spaghetti western" craze, who once announced at a party, in French, that, "Clint Eastwood has two expressions—one with his hat, and one without his hat."

I also became socially acquainted with the extraordinary film actress Michèle Morgan. She has too many acting credentials to even try to list them here, including a Best Actress award at the Cannes Film Festival, and she was utterly charming.

One night Michèle told the story of how she moved to Hollywood during World War II. She designed a French Country-style home to be built there, fairly private and only a short distance away from the heart of Beverly Hills where most other movie stars were living. But in time she was frightened to live there because she kept hearing what she described as "sinister noises," and she eventually sold the property.

The house Michèle Morgan built, the house full of "sinister noises" that frightened her, was 10050 Cielo Drive, my former residence and, of course, the house where the murders occurred. What are the odds that I would just happen to become acquainted with her, through a chance encounter with a Greek singer at an Athens I?

Thank you, Nana Mouskouri, for the introduction to Michèle and so many others, for inviting me to be a guest on your show and all the opportunities that invitation led to, and for being such a warm, generous friend who gave me memories of Paris I'll always treasure.

A movie in Spain called *Sharon vestida de rojo* (*Sharon in Scarlet*) . . . another movie in Spain and France called *The Day the Hot Line Got Hotter* with Charles Boyer and Robert Taylor. Back to the United States for some TV appearances. I was having a great time, and so busy that it caught me completely off guard when I got a call out of nowhere from my old *West Side Story* producer Hal Prince, whom I hadn't talked to in years.

After a minute or two of catching up and confirming that we were both fine, he got right to the point:

"How would you feel about playing the male lead in the national tour of *Company* with Elaine Stritch?"

Chapter Eleven

COMPANY WAS A STEPHEN SONDHEIM MUSICAL THAT HAD BEEN A SUC-cess on Broadway for a year. It was gearing up for a national tour. Elaine Stritch, star of the original Broadway cast, was joining the tour. *Elaine Stritch*. Yes, I *absolutely* wanted to be part of it.

Next thing I knew, there I was . . .

Preparing to perform Sondheim onstage in a hit musical produced by Hal Prince.

Renting an apartment in New York.

Taking the bus down Broadway for rehearsals at the Alvin Theatre.

Rehearsing with Ruth Mitchell, the stage manager for *West Side Story* at the Winter Garden Theater in 1958, the woman who sent me to audi-tion for Jerry Robbins.

In the words of the late, great Yogi Berra, it was like déjà vu all over again . . .

Almost.

Ruth Mitchell, that warm, friendly, always smiling woman who'd been so kind and supportive of me all those years ago, now seemed kind of sad and bitter. She was still a champion at her job, but she'd been transformed into a woman who would *never* smile or seem to be enjoying herself, who would stare sternly at her watch until everyone was there and glare at any-one who was even a minute late. I never knew, and certainly never asked her, what had brought on this obvious unhappiness, although I wondered if maybe being Hal's associate producer had taken its toll. Whatever it was, I was sorry for her but glad to be working with her again.

I rehearsed with the cast of the national company that would even-tually open at the Ahmanson Theatre in Los Angeles. The original cast, including Elaine, was still performing every night at the Alvin Theatre, an incredible collection of talent that included, in addition to Elaine Stritch, Donna McKechnie, Teri Ralston, Barbara Barrie, Larry Kert, and Charles Kimbrough. When Elaine left the New York company for the tour, she would be replaced by Jane Russell, so I rehearsed with Jane as she prepared to take over for Elaine on Broadway. She was quiet, very focused, and always had a gentleman with her for rehearsals, an agent or manager, I assumed, and preferable to being there alone. I didn't envy her being in the position of trying to fill Elaine Stritch's shoes and the inevitable comparisons the critics would make; but Jane was giving it all she had, and I admired her for it.

A remarkable woman named Marti Stevens had been cast in the role of Sarah for the national tour. She was extremely pretty, had a great voice, was as professional and conscientious as could be, and she also happened to be the daughter of the renowned studio executive Nicholas Schenck. Marti grew up in a world of show business royalty and knew and was loved by everyone, but she was never a name dropper, which I always appreciated about her.

Marti and I took to each other from Day One, and we became friends. More often than not, after a day of rehearsing, we headed straight to Forno's, a popular steakhouse near the stage door of the Alvin Theatre, to relax with a good glass of wine.

Hal Prince would drop in on rehearsals unexpectedly from time to time to see how things were going. One day, less than two weeks after we'd started, before we'd even done a run-through, he asked me if I'd like to perform in a matinee, probably to make sure I was learning the material fast enough. Whatever prompted him to ask, I said, "Sure!" Marti found out I was doing the matinee and asked if she could do it as well, and next thing we knew, we were on Broadway! For a whole matinee! We got through it completely unscathed! The cast and crew couldn't have been more supportive, encouraging and helping us through the performance and it was an unbelievably exciting afternoon.

Until Marti approached Ruth Mitchell and asked for some feedback. Ruth, within earshot of everyone backstage, shot back, "F**k off!" Nope, definitely not the Ruth Mitchell I knew back in the day. None of us could imagine where that outburst came from or what it was about, but it became apparent over time that there was no need for Marti to take it personally. Ruth once said to Elaine Stritch, "You know, you intimidate me," to which Elaine replied, "You're not exactly Howdy Doody yourself."

The first time I saw Elaine, I was coming through the stage door of the Alvin and there she was, visiting with the stagehands. We hadn't been introduced yet, so I didn't say anything. I just took note of the fact that she seemed to be living up to her reputation for knowing everyone in a production, onstage and off. I overheard someone say about her, "Don't invite Elaine to your house. She'll never leave." I didn't know what they meant by that, and I wasn't about to ask. It just sounded unkind, and it didn't deter me one bit from wanting to get to know her. I'm pleased to say that it didn't take long.

As I mentioned, Marti Stevens knew everyone, but she didn't make a big deal about it. So one night she invited me to join her at Forno's for an early dinner after rehearsal to meet a friend of hers who was in New York with a couple of friends of his. Her friend turned out to be Sir Noël Coward. I hadn't been in the same room with him that I knew of since the *West Side Story* opening night in London, and here I was, just him, Marti, and me, with a chance to actually get acquainted with him. I was thrilled.

Then, as if that weren't enough of a treat, Elaine Stritch came walking in and sat down at the table with us for a little while before heading on to the theater for her *Company* performance that night. She and Marti were already pals, and she and Noël Coward knew each other very well—she'd starred in *Sail Away* in London, a musical for which he wrote the book, the music, and the lyrics. I just sat quietly and listened to the three of them talk, basking in another one of those "I'm *where*?! With *who*?!" moments.

It was a typical early evening in a New York City winter, very cold, accompanied by occasional sleet. The poor hat check girl was in her little room, almost buried under an avalanche of raincoats, overcoats, scarves, hats, and umbrellas. Mr. Coward was sitting with his back to her, and at one point Elaine leaned over to him and said, "Noël, would you please turn around and say hello to the hat check girl? She's absolutely beside herself." He turned around, looked at the hat check girl, and then turned back to Elaine and said, "She's hardly got room [to be beside herself]!"

Good Lord, to have that quick a wit . . . or Elaine's laugh, for that matter, that seemed to come from somewhere deep inside her. I couldn't wait to work with her and get to know this woman.

Our rehearsals in New York finally came to an end, and we flew to Los Angeles to resume them at the Ahmanson Theatre.

I have to say, the hardest part of rehearsing at the Ahmanson was finding my car at the end of the day in that cavernous parking lot with occasional partitions here and there. I couldn't even count the number of times I scuffed into that lot, exhausted and just wanting to go home; looked everywhere for my car until I was convinced it had been towed; gave serious thought to calling a cab; and almost tearfully reunited with it when I finally found it hiding behind a partition.

Company, like everything Sondheim, is a challenging, exhilarating show to perform.

It's about a bachelor named Bobby (my character) living in New York City. His friends are all married or engaged couples. Among the married couples are Harry and Sarah (Marti) and Larry and Joanne (Elaine), and the theme is commitment, and the fear of it.

There's a major scene in Act II in which Joanne and Bobby (Elaine and me) are in a nightclub together drinking while watching her husband Larry dance. Joanne, drunkenly commenting on those who watch life rather than live it, scornfully toasts "The Ladies Who Lunch":

> Here's to the ladies who lunch
> Everybody laugh.
> Lounging in their caftans
> And planning a brunch
> On their own behalf . . .

It was a showstopper, and one of Elaine's career signature songs. She did it brilliantly, of course, although one night during a performance she noticed an unusually large number of women in the audience. She leaned over to me before she sang it and muttered, "Oh, they're going to hate me."

Before the scene ends, Joanne suggests that she and Bobby have an affair, promising that she'll take care of him. Bobby's reply, "But who will I take care of?", leads to an epiphany on his part, and his song "Being Alive":

> Someone to hold me too close.
> Someone to hurt me too deep.
> Someone to sit in my chair
> And ruin my sleep,
> And make me aware
> Of being alive . . .

Elaine always called it my "eleven o'clock number," which in theater parlance is a song near the end of the second act that precedes the story's loose ends being tied up. It's a great song. I looked forward to singing it night after night. One of the nicest compliments of my career came from Stephen Sondheim, who told me after a show, "That was the best 'Being Alive' I've ever heard."

On stage with Elaine Stritch in Company, 1971

Marti, Elaine, and I always spent time together after the show. I've heard more stories than I can count about Elaine's reputation for drinking, and she was certainly candid about it, including a lengthy discussion of it many years later in her one-woman show *Elaine Stritch at Liberty*. She openly admitted that she started drinking in her early teens and relied on alcohol to bolster her through stage fright and other insecurities. But I can honestly say that even though I did *Company* with her for almost a year, and socialized with her constantly, I never saw her drunk. Not once. She had a shot of brandy before the show, one at intermission, and one for her "eleven o'clock number," "The Ladies Who Lunch." Beyond that, she never had more than one glass of wine afterwards with Marti and me. It's always annoyed me when even the most respectful critics would refer to her "gin-soaked voice." She didn't have a gin-soaked voice, she had a *great* voice. Elaine Stritch's voice.

I've done a lot of theater in my life, but I've never seen anyone better, or more at home, or more honest onstage than Elaine. One night in our final scene together, one of her eyelashes came slightly unglued. Most actresses would have frozen a little and held their breath, praying that eyelash wouldn't fall off until the scene was over and she was safely back in the wings. Not Elaine. Without so much as a pause, she took off the loose eyelash, put it in the ashtray, then took off the other eyelash and put that one in the ashtray too, as if she were unwinding in her own living room after a long day. Honest. Brave. Unapologetic. I loved it that she showed up to our opening night party wearing hot pants, which were very "in" at the time. She was justifiably proud of her legs, and based on how she looked at that party, hot pants seemed to have been invented just for her.

It was while we were in L.A. that Elaine met an attractive guy her age and ended up spending the weekend. She was single at the time, and a consenting adult, so why not? She was telling me about it at the theater on Monday, without a hint of embarrassment, and I asked her if she'd had a good time. She kind of shrugged and said, "He told me he doesn't like oral sex. I told him I don't like to talk about it either." I've never known anyone more comfortable and unedited than Elaine when it came to telling stories about herself.

On one of our dark nights at the Ahmanson, a charity was using both the Ahmanson Theatre and the nearby Dorothy Chandler Pavilion for a major-league celebrity gala, starring every A-lister in the business from Streisand to Sinatra to Princess Grace to you name it. The stars would be using our dressing rooms, so the management asked us to please clear everything out, except for our rotary phones, which, of course, we locked every night when we left the theater.

It turned out that Barbra Streisand was going to be using Elaine's dressing room. Elaine left her a message in lipstick on the mirror, a long-stemmed rose in a nice vase, and a very classy card with a note inside.

She asked me who was using my dressing room. I had no idea, so Elaine asked around and found out: It was Princess Grace.

"You've got to leave her a note!" Elaine ordered.

It was a lovely idea, except for two small problems—I didn't have any note cards, and I wouldn't have the slightest idea what to say in a note to Her Serene Highness. Elaine gave me one of her cards and dictated the note I should write.

Princess Grace arrived on the night of the gala and walked into my dressing room to find nothing but a locked phone on the dressing table and a note beside it that read, thanks to Elaine, "Dear Princess Grace, Just in case you should need to call home, I've got the key."

Our almost one-year run in *Company* included seven weeks in San Francisco. Friends of mine were in town from London, and I had dinner plans with them after the show one night. I was getting ready to go onstage when Marti popped her head in my dressing room door and said, "A friend of mine is here tonight, and I'd love for you to join us for dinner after the show."

You'd think after the Noël Coward incident in New York, I would have hedged my bets and immediately changed my plans. But no. I explained about my friends from London, and she shrugged it off with a simple, "No problem. Another time," and left.

Minutes later I happened to notice a blonde figure pass by my open door, headed down the short corridor to Elaine's dressing room. It took

At home on Laurel Canyon, 1971

a few seconds for it to hit me—"Oh, my God, that's Dietrich! Of course! Marti's friend is Marlene Dietrich . . . and I just passed up a chance to have dinner with her?!"

Needless to say, I switched dinner with my London friends to another night and met Elaine, Marti, and Marlene at Trader Vic's. Marlene was very quiet, dressed in navy blue slacks and a matching jacket, with no makeup. I sat directly opposite her and made certain throughout the entire dinner that whenever I looked at her, I made direct eye contact. Elaine and Marti kept the conversation moving, and we all had a really good time. I was sorry when it ended and we all made the usual "good night, what a pleasure, we must do this again soon" noises. And somehow, in just a couple of hours, over one dinner, I'd managed to develop a massive crush on Marlene Dietrich.

I still can't believe I had the gall to call her at her hotel later that evening. I don't have a clue what I said, I just remember that she was very polite and that I felt embarrassed when I hung up and hoped I hadn't sounded too stupid. Looking back, I think she recognized the sincerity and shyness in my voice and responded with nothing but kindness. I was like a schoolboy in love.

The next night I was in my dressing room getting ready for the show when she stuck her head in the door. Yes, it was *her*, stopping by to announce that she'd decided to stay another night. So for two nights in a row, we had Dietrich watching *Company* from the wings. It was impossible not to think about it from time to time while I was onstage, and it was the one and only performance when I was sorry that my character, Bobby, was rarely offstage for the entire show.

It happened to be my dresser John's birthday that evening. He told me later that she'd said to him, "If I had known it was your birthday I would have gotten you something." He told her that the perfect birthday present would be for her to allow herself to be introduced to the audience in a special curtain call.

So . . . final curtain call. Elaine stepped forward, and the audience quieted down to hear her. She said something like, "We have someone who's been with us for the past two nights, cleaning the dressing rooms, and sweeping the stage, etc." She then raised her left arm upstage toward me, and Dietrich stepped out from behind the curtain and stood right next to me, just the two of us on the upper platform. (Where was the photographer when I needed him?!) Elaine never said her name. She didn't need to, although Dietrich later told her she should have. The audience instantly went crazy, recognizing that beautiful woman, a knockout in her slacks, peacoat, and flats, with just a little lipstick and her hair fluffed. In a simple curtain call, Marlene Dietrich gave the audience, and us, a great reason to be in the theater that night.

Then, *Company* was over for the evening. Now what?

Elaine, Marti, Dietrich, our stage manager Ben Strobach, and I went across the street to a cozy piano bar/restaurant that was frequented by performers after their respective shows. We made our way through the crowded room to a small banquette in the back, where, with no manipulating on my part, I got to sit next to Dietrich—a big deal when you're in love. At one point she excused herself from the table, walked over to the piano and sang "Lili Marlene," a signature German love song of hers, to a hushed, enthralled private audience. Marti whispered to me, "She never does that," and I was silently honored that she was feeling so comfortable with us that night.

It was getting late. Elaine and Ben ordered turkey sandwiches to take back to the hotel in case room service was closed by the time they got there. When the waiter brought the sandwiches, Dietrich immediately confiscated Elaine's and gave it to me, with the explanation to Elaine that, "He works very hard." I ate every bite of that sandwich, hungry or not; and I did the same thing when Dietrich handed me Ben's sandwich as well. It was the first and only time I ever ate two turkey sandwiches after a show, but under the circumstances, how could I not?

Before that night was over, Dietrich had also given me a beautiful bottle of Courvoisier and a note, both of which I cherished for a very long time. She also told me to come by sometime so she could cook for me. She left San Francisco the next day. Nothing romantic ever happened between us, and I only saw her once more, when I went to see her one-woman show, *An Evening with Marlene Dietrich*, at the Ahmanson. But the legendary Dietrich will always have a place in my heart reserved just for her, not only for her magnetic presence as a woman and a movie star, but also for being the great unconsummated crush of my life.

Company left San Francisco not long after Dietrich did. We moved on to Toronto, where one of our top priorities when we got there was getting tickets to see Liza Minnelli at the O'Keefe Center on our first dark night. Needless to say, Liza had come a long way from that precious ten-year-old girl I met when I was working with her mom Judy Garland in Las Vegas. All the superlative adjectives have already been used to describe Liza's live performances, and she lived up to every one of them at that show.

Elaine, Marti, and I attended a big party that was thrown for Liza that night. Fabulous.

As a guest on her show with the lovely Dinah Shore, 1971

Of course someone pleaded, "Liza, please sing!"

Liza sang and the room was enthralled. Then Elaine kind of transitioned into a hostess role and sang/talked an incredibly touching rendition of "I've Grown Accustomed to His Face." Finally, not to be outdone, as if she could ever be, Marti sang, doing her uncanny impressions of Marlene Dietrich and Judy Garland, which took particular guts with Liza Minnelli looking on. When she finished, to rousing cheers and applause, Elaine turned to her and said, "Gee, Marti, won't it be great when you can do yourself?"

Anyone who knew Elaine knew she wasn't one to hold her tongue. It was one of her most renowned assets, or liabilities if you were too thin-skinned. She wasn't gossipy, and she probably had a filter; she just didn't choose to use it very often. But she was accurate and always hit the nail on the head with her uncanny perceptions!

When she and I first started doing *Company* together, she noticed that my dressing room door was always closed, while she took pride in the fact that hers was always open. One night before a show she stopped by my dressing room to pour herself a shot of my brandy, since she'd run out of hers. She started out the door, then opened it again part-way and asked, with meaning, "Are you sure you want this closed?" I just looked at her and said, "Yes, please," since it was such a rhetorical question. So she added, "You think this has anything to do with your performance?" Well, that made me laugh and I left my dressing room door open from that night on.

At the beginning of the second act of *Company*, I was standing upstage behind a table with a birthday cake. Elaine was seated with her back to the audience. One night as the candles were being lit and the curtain was about to go up, Elaine looked up at me and said, "Jesus Christ, you look just like Jane Fonda." I was still struggling to stop laughing when the curtain rose.

I loved that woman.

And I loved doing *Company*. It was truly a joy.

Until it wasn't.

Chapter Twelve

HAL GAVE A CLOSING NIGHT DINNER FOR THE CAST AT TRADER VIC'S IN San Francisco.

As we were walking into the restaurant Ben Strobach, our stage manager, told me that Hal wanted to talk to me.

I was intrigued, wondering if maybe Hal was going to ask me to join the upcoming London production of *Company*.

But no. Instead, after dinner, as we were about to leave Trader Vic's, Hal stepped up and said, almost off-handedly, "Would you mind if I cut the dance in 'Side By Side'?"

That caught me off-guard, and I didn't hear the word "London" in there; so without even thinking, I just said, "Oh. Sure."

I regretted that answer the minute we started rehearsals Monday morning in Toronto.

"Side By Side By Side" is Bobby's (my) opening number in *Company*. The scene is Bobby's birthday party, in a nightclub, and he's reflecting on the fact that his being best friends with couples means he's always a third wheel:

> Isn't it warm?
> Isn't it rosy?
> Side by side by side.
> Ports in a storm,
> Comfy and cozy,
> Side by side by side . . .

Michael Bennett, the show's brilliant choreographer, who was instrumental in making *Company* the huge success it was, created a wonderful dance sequence for me for "Side By Side By Side," a sequence I really enjoyed. So I was in nothing short of shock when we started rehearsing that Monday and the impact of Hal's question finally hit me. "Would you mind if I cut the dance in 'Side By Side'?" My answer should have been, "Yes, I would mind. Very much."

It seems some friends of Hal's had seen the show in San Francisco and told him they thought the dance wasn't necessary. And that meant it was out? Just like that? Michael Bennett had added the dance after I started doing *Company*. He thought it was necessary and enhanced the song and Bobby's dilemma. The first time Elaine saw it she said, "That's how it should have been in the first place." But the off-hand opinion of a few of Hal's friends over dinner or drinks, friends who'd probably seen the show exactly once, carried more weight with him than the opinions of Michael Bennett, Elaine Stritch, and me? What possible sense did that make? For what possible artistic reason?

I was already unhappy enough about that. But then Hal presented me with his reconfigured concept for the song itself.

The gorgeous original set I'd always worked on, a set that got its own rave reviews, included actual working elevators. Some of the couples in the scene, Bobby's friends, would use the elevators to get to the upper platform, while I stayed on the stage level for the whole song and dance.

In Toronto, though, we were using the bus and truck tour set, a scaled-down version of the original. Understandably, there wasn't an elevator. There was just an awkward configuration of two staircases with lots and lots of steps that were connected at the top by the upper level of the set.

Hal's bright idea was to cut the dance and replace it by having me sing "Side By Side By Side" while going up the steps stage left, move across the upper level, and come back down the steps stage right. To navigate the stairs while playing to the audience, do justice to the phrasing of Sondheim's song, and give a performance was a mess. It felt forced and awkward and contrived. I'll happily take on a challenge any day of the week, but only if I understand the point, and wow, did I not understand the point.

To make sure I wasn't out of line and getting upset for no legitimate reason, I talked to Elaine about it. She agreed with me and strongly encouraged me to discuss it with Hal. So I went to him and asked him why. Why cut the dance? Why not leave it in, let me perform it and the song on the stage level as always, and spare me and the audience that gratuitous nonsense on the stairs?

The first time I very politely asked, he brushed me off. To be fair, he was busy rehearsing the show on an unfamiliar, scaled-down set, with our opening night in Toronto just hours away.

I backed off, temporarily.

"Talk to him again," Elaine said. I assured her I had every intention of it.

The second time I asked, not quite as politely, he pretty much ignored me.

The third time, I'd run out of patience, and so had he.

"Hal, why . . . ?!"

He turned, looked me right in the eye, and spat back, "Because I'm the producer!"

And that was that . . . I walked away.

I have my limits, but I was angry. I worked hard all day on making the song work while maneuvering those steps, believing with all my heart that losing the dance was a big mistake and that the audience was being cheated out of a great Michael Bennett sequence. Opening night went well, and we all gathered as always for Hal's notes after the performance. I listened to him, but at that moment, I really didn't like this guy, and I couldn't look at him.

I worked hard on that number on Tuesday as well. In the end, like it or not, it was my job to "sell it," and finally I did manage to smooth it out. I could have made it look as idiotic as I thought it was, just to prove a point to Hal. There's an old saying, though, that revenge is like drinking poison and expecting the other person to die. I wasn't about to make a fool of myself onstage in the hope of forcing Hal to see the error of his ways, apologize, and tell me I was right to begin with, and either put the dance back in or let me stay on stage level to sing that song.

By Wednesday, not only had I perfected my way around that set and all those stairs, but I was also fine. I wasn't angry at Hal anymore. In fact, I was over the whole thing and looking forward to our performance that night . . . which turned out to be one of the more bizarre nights of my life onstage.

In our last scene together, Joanne (Elaine) and Bobby (me) are having drinks at a small table in the discotheque while her husband and our friends are all dancing. Joanne, who's drunk, says to Bobby, "When are we gonna make it?" Bobby doesn't exactly leap at the invitation.

During those lines of dialogue, Joanne takes out a fresh pack of cigarettes, tears open one side of the top, and very expertly taps the bottom of the pack so that three or four cigarettes pop up, making it easy for her to pull one out. Then she drops the pack of cigarettes on the table for soft emphasis on her line, "Because you're weak."

On that particular Wednesday night, when Elaine picked up the fresh pack of cigarettes, she must have torn off the whole top of the pack; on the line, "Because you're weak," she somehow hit the bottom of it with the palm of her hand and sent the whole pack—twenty loose cigarettes—flying all over the stage.

It was obviously unplanned and obviously out of character. It shocked the cast. It even shocked the audience. And it shocked the absolute hell out of me.

We finished the scene without another incident, but I was still upset, completely thrown, when I was back in my dressing room after the performance. What on earth had happened? What on earth had caused one of the most professional actors who ever graced a stage to do something so clearly unprofessional, so clearly wrong?

For the first time in our year of working together and becoming friends, I found it impossible to say good night to Elaine when I left the theater that night, even though we had adjoining dressing rooms. She didn't say good night to me either.

The next night we didn't say hello or good night. Same thing the night after that. The tension was building. Our last scene together proceeded as rehearsed, for the most part. I'd always deferred to her in that scene, without really being aware of it, because I loved her and had such respect for her. But I'm guessing that because of her momentary outburst, followed by no explanation and no apology, I allowed myself not to worry or care or give a damn about what Elaine thought of me or my work. It must have caused a subtle change in the dynamics in the scene between Joanne and Bobby, because she was suddenly getting unexpected chuckles from the audience that she didn't like one bit and apparently blamed me for.

It was on about night number four after the cigarettes-on-the-floor incident that Elaine burst into my dressing room and announced, in tears, "One of us has to go!"

My first impulse was to go to her and put my arms around her. She was so distraught, so distressed, and I really wanted to help her, even though it somehow involved me. She didn't want my help at the moment, nor did she even want to talk about it. She just left.

Very slowly but surely the tension between us eased. In the end, neither of us had to go. Our last scene together went back to normal, and we started saying hello and good night and being comfortable dressing room neighbors again. Neither of us ever mentioned her bizarre flash of temper, or whatever it was, onstage. I never asked her what happened or why, or if it had anything to do with my brief dispute with Hal—I couldn't imagine how those two incidents might be connected, but since they occurred two days apart, it did cross my mind once or twice. I'd missed my friend, and I was just glad that we seemed to be back on track.

Unfortunately, though, those more-than-a-few nights when Elaine and I weren't speaking took a weird toll on me. One morning at about 4:00 or 5:00 a.m. my mouth suddenly felt so strange and uncomfortable that it actually woke me up. I got out of bed and hurried to the bathroom mirror, and I may have literally gasped—my lips, which had been perfectly normal when I went to sleep, were so painfully, grotesquely swollen that I looked as if someone had come in during the night and turned them inside out. I immediately tracked down the stage manager, got to a doctor, and, and, and. . . .

I'd never had that kind of reaction to stress before, and it really alarmed me. I missed a couple of performances, which I *hated* and felt guilty about, but it took that long for the swelling to go down and for me not to look like a science experiment that had gone horribly wrong. I missed a few more performances when this random facial swelling launched a surprise attack out of nowhere. With no warning, I'd wake up every once in a while with those same swollen lips, or a perfectly symmetrical swollen jaw line the size of Texas, definitely not ready for my closeup, let alone two and a half hours onstage, unless Hal came up with some reason to explain why Bobby had taken to wearing a bag on his head. I lived in fear of waking up swollen, which of course exacerbated my stress, which of course exacerbated my occasional swelling . . . while Elaine, by the way, was perfectly fine and never missed a single performance.

We were in Ohio for Thanksgiving, and the *Company* management threw us a very nice, traditional Thanksgiving dinner. I was briefly out of the show again that night, but I did join my castmates for that dinner—they weren't bothered by how temporarily disfigured my face was when there was a Thanksgiving feast to focus on. Things were still a little tense between Elaine and me. She was talking about doing the show in Florida, and I heard myself say, "That's great, Elaine, we could spray your legs pink and you could be a flamingo." Not my finest moment, but I guess I have a mean streak in me when I'm a stressed-out, swollen mess and my last nerve gets used up.

My exit from *Company* turned out to be complicated. The national tour was ending in Philadelphia, and the bus and truck tour was about to begin. I hadn't signed on for the bus and truck tour. No one in the cast had signed on for the bus and truck tour—a mistake by the people who worked for Hal and were responsible for drawing up our initial contracts. Hal would have been furious with them if he'd found that out, and I don't doubt for a moment that they were all terrified enough of him that they were praying he never did.

Bearing that in mind, imagine my surprise. . . . We were performing in Philadelphia when I was informed that Hal was suing me for not doing the bus and truck tour I'd never committed to. It had to be a mistake. But unbelievably, it wasn't.

I immediately hired attorney Arnold Weissberger.

While I was pacing and agonizing and steaming over this outrageous turn of events, I thought back to a seemingly trivial moment when we were doing *Company* in San Francisco. I arrived in my dressing room one night to find a single sheet of paper on the table. I asked Ben Strobach what it was. He nonchalantly replied, "Oh, it's just something Equity wants you to sign."

Apparently the truthful answer would have been, "Oh, Hal's people forgot to include an agreement to do the bus and truck tour in your original contract, so they need you to sign this rider to keep them out of trouble with Hal."

I had a show to get ready for, so I only glanced at the sheet of paper, got a vague gist of it, and set it aside without signing it. The next day I sent it on to Ruth Aarons, who told me she passed it along to my agent at the William Morris Agency, and I honestly never gave it another thought until I found myself on the receiving end of a lawsuit from Hal Prince.

The case went to arbitration, and off I went on the train from Philadelphia to an office in New York. There we sat with the arbitrator at a very large table—me, my attorney, and the Equity lawyers on one side, Ruth Mitchell and Bobby Fisher, who was responsible for Hal's contracts, on the other.

At some point the arbitrator mentioned that he thought Ruth Aarons knew about the bus and truck mix-up, but she was conspicuously absent from my side of the table.

Somehow, in spite of all the facts being on my side and Equity's full support, the arbitrator ended up ruling in Hal's favor. I was livid, and so convinced it was an unfair political ruling that I wondered if Hal had paid off the arbitrator, or at least influenced him. The decision was final, though, and I owed Hal a settlement of $5,000, which Ruth Aarons convinced the William Morris Agency to pay.

I finished my *Company* contract and agreed to do two weeks of the bus and truck to give them time to find a replacement. Even though none of us in the national tour had committed to do the bus and truck, some of my castmates were happy to do it. Work is work, after all, and a great show is a great show. Those of us who never intended to do that tour in the first place, like Elaine and me, had simply made other plans and were ready to move on. Elaine's role on the new tour was being taken over by a fine actress and singer named Julie Wilson, and it was my pleasure to work with her and help her prepare for the fantastic experience I knew she had ahead of her.

I remember Hal quietly saying to me during the break at the first of those rehearsals with Julie Wilson, "I don't think you knew [you'd signed on for the bus and truck tour], but I think Ruth Aarons did." Exactly what the arbitrator had said, but at that point, what difference did it make? Hal won, because Hal *had* to win, because "*I'm the producer!*" I had two choices: I could fight it and appeal it and obsess over it for God knows how long, or I could preserve my sanity, let it go, and move on.

I let it go and moved on, and I've never regretted it.

And I have to say that, looking back, the turbulence and drama of my final weeks with *Company* and the way it ended were *far* outweighed by the joy of doing it, of performing Sondheim again, and of getting to know and work with and love Marti, our whole fantastic team, and, of course, Elaine.

Happily, Elaine and I never moved on from each other. I saw her many times after *Company*, and not once did that rough patch between us ever even come up.

We got together in Paris when we found ourselves there at the same time.

I went four times to the Ahmanson Theatre to see her one-woman show *Elaine Stritch at Liberty*, and saw her backstage every time.

We saw each other many times in London after she met and married John Bay and they were living at the Savoy.

She tracked me down when I was in Chicago doing a special performance of *I Do, I Do* with Carol Lawrence, and she was there doing a commercial. I have no idea how she knew I was in Chicago; but she found me, and we got together to talk about life and its complete unpredictability. She and John had been happily married for nine years, and she was thriving in one successful theater production after another in the West End. And then she lost him when he died of a brain tumor at the age of fifty-three. She ended up leaving London, moving back to New York, and eventually relocating to Birmingham, Michigan, to a house she had built there. Proof that life can definitely be unfair.

I was so touched that she'd sought me out and confided in me about some very personal feelings. It wasn't something she did easily or randomly.

My heart broke for her, but she didn't want my comforting hugs, or my sympathy, she just wanted me there. Me. And that meant the world to me.

Elaine, you were one of a kind. I miss you, I will always love you, and I cherish the fact that you and your irrepressible spirit were part of my life.

After *Company* I played El Gallo in *The Fantastiks* at Dallas Summer Theater Musicals, 1972.

Chapter Thirteen

WORK TOOK ME TO LONDON AGAIN, AS IF I NEEDED AN EXCUSE TO GO. IT was great to be back. That city has always been so good to me, and it's always brought me almost uncanny luck. This trip was no exception.

Before I'd even left the States, I was talking to a good friend named Ed Wassall, a designer and photographer, and mentioned that I was headed to London and needed to find a place to rent. Ed just happened to know someone who had a flat there that he wasn't using at the time. Maybe I knew him—Richard Chamberlain. I didn't, but I'd certainly be happy to. Richard and I talked, and what do you know, he was as glad to have a paying tenant in his flat as I was to be one. I arrived in London with a job in hand and an already arranged place to stay, a place that turned out to be a beautiful two-story flat in Hyde Park Gardens with a spectacular view of the park itself.

The job was an episode of the British anthology series *Thriller* that aired in the United States under the ABC Wide World of Entertainment banner. Each episode was a self-contained story. In my episode, "Kiss Me and Die," my character traveled from America to an English village in search of my brother, who seemed to have suddenly vanished into thin air. I had a terrific time, highlighted by the opportunity to get to know and work with a very special young actress named Jenny Agutter.

When I wasn't working, I was enjoying my reunion with London's warm social life, particularly Sunday lunches at the homes of a variety of charming, gracious English theater people. When I finished working on "Kiss Me and Die," Irene Finch, my terrific London agent and friend, suggested it would be nice for me to reciprocate and host a Sunday lunch at my/Richard's place before I went back to the States, to thank everyone who'd been so generous to me for all those weeks.

It was obviously a perfect idea, and exactly the right thing to do. There was only one problem—I'm pretty good at being a guest, but I've never been gifted at being a good host. I don't have the first clue where to start or what to have on hand for everyone to eat and drink. What if I serve something my guests don't like, or someone's allergic to? Music? No music? If there is music, *what* music? What do I do if people get bored . . . ? I go on and on with a thousand uncertainties, and I can break out in a cold sweat just thinking about it.

Not to worry. Irene happened to be brilliant at entertaining. She took charge of everything from the invitations to the cooking, table settings, and decorating, and she did it masterfully. She assembled a funny, comfortable, stimulating group of people; and apparently everyone was enjoying themselves as much as I was, since most of them were still there at 1:00 a.m., twelve hours after the party started.

One of the people Irene strongly suggested I invite was a man named Pieter Rogers. He was a producer at the BBC. He'd helped Sir Laurence Olivier create the esteemed Chichester Theatre Festival and spent years as the general manager of the Royal Court Theatre. He knew everyone in the theater community; but far more impressive than that was his reputation not only as a talented producer but also as an incredible friend. He was widely sought after for career advice, with an extraordinary gift for connecting with people on all levels. He was such a fantastic problem solver that people walked away after talking to him feeling as if there was never really a problem to begin with. He was kind, he was loyal, and he'd do anything he could to help someone, personally and professionally.

Of *course* we should invite him. Who wouldn't want to get to know someone like that?

And to my amazement, he came!

At some point during the twelve-hour lunch, Pieter started talking about a project he was working on for the BBC, the miniseries *Notorious Woman*, about the French novelist George Sand. Out of nowhere, he tossed in, "You might be very good as the Italian doctor." It wasn't some polite, empty way of throwing a bone to the party host. He clearly meant it. I'm sure I responded with something like, "Thank you, that sounds great," but I honestly didn't start planning on it. Sincere as he seemed at the moment, you learn pretty early in this business not to take cocktail party job offers too seriously.

I was back in L.A. a couple of months later when Pieter called from London. The BBC had given a green light to *Notorious Woman*, but he no longer wanted me to play the Italian doctor. He wanted me to play Frédéric Chopin instead.

Out of the blue—Chopin! What a fantastic opportunity. Chopin, of course, was the legendary Polish composer and virtuoso pianist, a true musical genius. He was also one of the most significant affairs of George Sand's life. I'd be in four episodes of the seven-episode miniseries. Was I interested? Yes. Or, to be more precise, *yes*!

I immediately signed a contract with the BBC and drove straight to the UCLA library to start reading books on Chopin and George Sand. I was pretty good at reading music, so I also rented a piano and taught myself to play one of Chopin's études. I woke up every morning excited to get out of bed and work on this role. We were filming later that year, and I wanted to be ready.

It didn't hit me at first, but at some point I realized what an extraordinary imagination it took for Pieter to even think of me as Frédéric Chopin in *Notorious Woman*. He never asked me to read, or test. He simply offered me the role on pure gut instinct and trusted me to pull it off. Not all producers have that kind of imagination. It's a real gift, in this case both to Pieter and to me, and I have always been grateful for it.

Then came a call about another project that sounded almost too good to be true. It seems the legendary theatrical producer David Merrick, aka God, was casting a show called *Dancers*. Tony Award–winning theatrical choreographer/director Ron Field would be directing. And Robert Joffrey, co-founder of the world-renowned Joffrey Ballet, would choreograph. They were interested in me for the role of a dancer who'd suffered an injury and couldn't dance anymore. In other words, a dramatic role, not a dancing role, led by Merrick, Field, and Joffrey, a team of superstars. Yes, I definitely wanted in on that!

I flew to New York to audition for David Merrick and Ron Field. They were considering Mary Jo Catlett, an absolute delight, for the female lead and had the two of us read together. It was kind of an eerie atmosphere—a total of four people in an otherwise empty theater, Merrick and Field in the house, Mary Jo and me on the stage. They told us to take some time onstage, work on the scene, and then let them know when we were ready. About twenty minutes later we decided we were as ready as we were going to get. But Merrick and Field had been watching us prepare and interact, and it turned out we didn't need to read after all. They'd already decided they wanted both of us for *Dancers*. It was thrilling, there's no other word for it.

So now I had *Notorious Woman* for the BBC and *Dancers* for David Merrick to look forward to, with signed contracts for both projects. Wow. Life was great . . . I thought.

Not long after the contracts were signed, I got the dates for the two projects. Unbelievably, they directly conflicted with each other. In an instant I went from ecstatic to torn up—it suddenly looked as if I couldn't do both projects, no matter how much I wanted to. And I *really* wanted to!

I was determined to see if there was any way that something could be worked out, so I called Ruth Aarons, my trusty manager, explained the situation, and asked her what I should do.

As far as she was concerned, it was a no-brainer. David Merrick was David Merrick, and he was far more important than "some BBC thing."

She wasn't getting it. I didn't want to have to choose between them, I wanted her to intervene and see if she could make that happen somehow. Besides . . .

"Ruth, I've already signed a contract with the BBC for the Pieter Rogers miniseries. What do I do about that?"

Her answer took my breath away: "Let the BBC sue you."

I may have been naïve about the business, but this time I knew "wrong" when I heard it.

Finally, after a couple of days of agonizing and no sleep, I did the only thing I could think of—I picked up the phone, called Pieter Rogers and Ron Field, and told them about the dilemma.

It was a good lesson in honesty, and in dealing with reasonable people. They couldn't have been nicer, calmer, and more understanding. By the time the two conversations had ended, Pieter had given me a firm stop date for the miniseries, and Ron Field had simply adjusted the beginning of rehearsals for *Dancers* to accommodate that stop date.

I could do both projects after all. Just like that. Problem solved, drama over.

The punch line was that, as luck or fate would have it, *Dancers*, the David Merrick project, was never done. In other words, if I'd listened to Ruth's impulsive advice, I would have ended up with neither job and a lawsuit from the BBC.

None of which is to make the point that I was right and Ruth was wrong. It's just to make the point that impulsivity can create needless problems, and that following your instincts in the direction of honesty and integrity can lead to happy endings.

In this case, my happy ending was the joy of doing *Notorious Woman*.

To the surprise of no one, Pieter had assembled an incredible cast. Rosemary Harris as George Sand. Georgina Hale as George's rebellious daughter Solange. A relative newcomer named Jeremy Irons as Franz Liszt. Cathleen Nesbitt as Madame Dupin. Sinéad Cusack as the actress Marie Dorval. The embarrassment of riches went on and on; and from the very first day, I was so proud to be a part of it.

Rosemary Harris was given a Lifetime Achievement award at the 2019 Tony Awards. Hers really *is* a lifetime of achievement. What an amazing film and theatrical resume. I'm still disappointed that I missed seeing her and Elaine Stritch in Edward Albee's *A Delicate Balance* at Lincoln Center. It must have been unforgettable to see those two very powerful, very different actresses together onstage.

After playing opposite her in four of the seven parts of *Notorious Woman*, I feel perfectly qualified to say that Rosemary Harris is one of the deepest, most intelligent actresses I've ever had the pleasure of working with. She was always moving, with subtlety and grace. I don't believe she ever took the easy way out in anything she did. She was much too thoughtful for that; and if your work is as profound as Rosemary's, there *is* no easy way out—she just always made it *look* easy. One of the signs of a truly great artist, and that she most certainly is.

With Rosemary Harris in *Notorious*

So there I was, playing Chopin to a truly great artist's George Sand, and God bless her, from our first moment together to our last, she was incredibly respectful of me and everyone else, and of each actor's process.

Georgina Hale as Solange was so terrific. A few people commented on her "personality." She definitely has one, and it's a glorious advantage. As a person and an actress, she can never be accused of being boring.

I watched Georgina's first day of filming, and it was fascinating. She was doing a scene with Rosemary. Waris Hussein, our director, had already spent a good deal of time filming with Rosemary, and perhaps he'd become too familiar with her. I don't know exactly what was going on. But he seemed to be quite taken with Georgina and the fresh, exciting energy and talent she brought to the set on that first day. I think he found it refreshing and even a little seductive—not consciously, to be fair. As Georgina and Rosemary's scene progressed, it was subtly becoming off-balance. Through no deliberate effort on Georgina's part, it was becoming her scene, not Rosemary's, which was clearly not the writer's intention. Rosemary noticed. She didn't stop the scene, or say a thing to either Waris or Georgina. She just artfully, patiently, and singlehandedly brought the scene and its focus back where it belonged, with only a quiet suggestion here and there. She didn't make a fuss. I don't think there was any "make a fuss" in Rosemary.

It was extraordinary to watch it happen, and to watch the grace with which it happened. As far as I'm concerned, anyone who came away from working with Rosemary Harris without learning something valuable about their craft simply wasn't paying attention.

In the end, all of us, including Rosemary, were very proud of *Notorious Woman*. It aired twice on PBS in the United States and got great audience response. I take it as a much-appreciated compliment when, from time to time, someone feels compelled to approach me to say how much they loved *Notorious Woman* and never even mentions *West Side Story*.

I also found a friend for life in Pieter Rogers. We remained in frequent touch from then on, and I stayed at his flat many times when I was in London. I still smile remembering a gorgeous photo on a side table in the guest room at Pieter's. It was a shot of his treasured friend Vivien Leigh, whom I got to meet through him.

Pieter passed away in 2006. I was just one of the many, many people who were fortunate enough to be close to that wise, generous, loyal, imaginative, gifted man. We all miss him.

Chapter Fourteen

Writing about Pieter Rogers makes me stop, think, and really marvel at how blessed a reserved man like me has been to have such extraordinary friends all over the world, including right here at home in L.A. You've probably caught on by now that I've never been one to be socially aggressive, but I did seek people out and managed to have such a busy, active social life that I actually envied myself. And in a way, it all started with Juliet Prowse.

Juliet and I weren't close friends, but we were often in dance class together. We did have a close mutual friend, though, named Maggie Banks, who was Jerry Robbins's camera assistant on *West Side Story*.

Maggie and Juliet were both working on different shows at NBC. I went to visit Maggie there one day, and the three of us got a chance to visit during a break. Juliet was involved with Frank Sinatra at the time. He wanted her to give up her career, which she clearly had no intention of doing. She was a very strong, independent woman. I remember her showing us a beautiful diamond necklace Sinatra had given her, and she treated it with humorous but complete disdain, as if it were paste.

Juliet had tickets to Engelbert Humperdinck's opening night at the Greek Theater, but a conflict came up and she couldn't go, so she gave the tickets to Maggie and me. After the concert we happened to run into my doctor Milton Uhley and his date, who'd arranged the whole evening, and they insisted we join them at the reception that was being held at the Bistro in Beverly Hills after the performance.

We'd only been at the reception for a few minutes when a very attractive, very gracious Englishwoman, who was there with her soon-to-be husband Vincente Minnelli, stepped over to me with the loveliest smile and said, "Oh, how nice to see you again."

I liked her immediately, so I wasn't about to point out that we'd actually never met.

It was thanks to Juliet Prowse's generosity with her Greek Theater concert tickets, followed by a simple, somewhat inaccurate introduction at the Bistro, that an incredible friendship formed between me and Lee Anderson Minnelli. She took it upon herself to make sure I was always invited to the best parties, introduced to all the A-list people, and mentioned very favorably in the press.

Lee and Vincente lived in a mansion at Sunset Boulevard and Crescent Drive in Beverly Hills. It was a gorgeous gathering place where I found myself on countless evenings, surrounded by the likes of Eva Gabor, Cyd Charisse, Fred Astaire, Vincent's daughter/Lee's stepdaughter Liza Minnelli, and an endless parade of other Hollywood royalty. It was a compliment to Lee and Vincent that there was no stuffiness or pretense at those gatherings. Everyone was relaxed, comfortable, and "themselves" in that home the minute they walked through the door.

I had the honor of escorting Lee to the film premiere of *Cabaret*, where I sat next to Liza. I knew what an important and exciting evening this was for Liza, and I was thrilled to be sitting next to Sally Bowles!

I escorted Lee to a Christmas party at Frank Sinatra's house. George Burns, in a wheelchair, was just leaving when we arrived. A sound system had been set up in the living room, with two microphones on stands, a pianist, a bass player, and a drummer. Eydie Gormé was already at the mike singing when we arrived. By the end of the evening, everyone got up and sang, including, incredibly, me, which speaks volumes about how much at ease all those people made me feel. Lee and I sat with Frank and Barbara Sinatra for dinner, and it was touching to watch how devoted and attentive Barbara was to him. At one point Frank leaned over to me and quietly said, "If there's anything you ever need, just let me know." Wow. I never took him up on it, but wow. Later in the evening we all gathered around the piano and sang some great standards together, songs we all knew, and I'll always remember how much more special that evening felt because of the music. The party was over by 11:30. We'd all had so much fun that, tired as we were, we were reluctant to leave. A few hours later, at 3:00 a.m. Christmas morning, we learned that Dean Martin, Sinatra's old

In concert in Tokyo in 1975

Rat Pack buddy, known and adored by Frank and everyone else at that party, had passed away.

I met Joanne Carson, Johnny's second wife, at a celebrity fashion show. We got friendly right away, and she started inviting me to her gatherings. She moved in her own dazzling social circle. Joanne kept a writing room for her close friend and confidant Truman Capote at her house, and it was at her house that he died in 1984. She had a New Year's Eve party every year: Phyllis Diller, Michael Feinstein, Betty White, Esther Williams, just a long, perfect guest list. Joanne always decorated the living room for the occasion with white helium balloons that covered the ceiling. A white ribbon was tied to each balloon, with a blank card attached to the ribbon. I remember Esther asking Joanne what the cards were for. Joanne reminded her that they were for each of us to write a special note to a loved one who'd passed on.

With Betty White at a party at Johnny Carson's, 1992

Michael Feinstein, Roddy McDowell, Joanne Carson, me, and Estelle Getty at Joanne's home, 1994

With the wonderful Phyllis Diller at Joanne Carson's home, 1995

"You know," Joanne told her, "like Fernando [Lamas, Esther's late husband]."

To which Esther replied, "Well, he never listened to me while he was here, why would he listen to me now?"

Joanne had a gift for coming up with special holiday traditions like those white balloons at the great gatherings she held at her home throughout the year. A night of having us come over to carve pumpkins was her way of getting ready for Halloween.

She was also a great animal lover. When I got my first rescue Italian Greyhound Sami, she helped with everything from sending me to the right veterinarian to giving me a corral for him while he was still getting acquainted with his new home. You couldn't ask for a more generous, loyal friend. She was always there for the people she loved, and I considered myself very fortunate to be one of them.

It was fun, and it was exciting to find myself surrounded by so many warm, welcoming people. It wasn't possible to develop close relationships with all of them; but as luck would have it, Phyllis Diller and I became very close friends. Phyllis was special, an amazing woman. So intelligent, so funny, of course, and most importantly, so genuinely nice—I really loved her!

Some years later I met Johnny Carson's next wife, Joanna, at the home of Janet de Cordova and her husband Fred, who was executive producing *The Tonight Show* at the time. It was so interesting to watch Johnny Carson at parties—he was obviously a gifted humorist, conversationalist, and host on television for thirty years. When I was a guest on *The Tonight Show*, he was masterful at pulling me out of my shyness and putting me at ease. But at the many social gatherings he and I both attended, including that night at the Cordovas', he was even more introverted than I was and always looked to me as if he couldn't wait to get out of there and head home.

As stimulating as that dinner party was, though, the highlight of the evening for me was meeting Jack Benny's widow Mary Livingstone, and I considered it a privilege that Janet asked me to pick up Jack's wife of almost fifty years and drive her home. I *loved* Jack Benny. I used to listen to his radio program after school when I was a kid, and my sister Viola and I got to attend one of his radio shows at CBS Studios on Sunset Boulevard. He was sponsored by Lucky Strike Cigarettes, and before the show he came out to talk to his audience, smoking a cigar. Being his widow's chauffeur that night seemed like a small way of repaying Jack Benny for all the laughter he added to my life.

And then, thanks yet again to Lee Minnelli, there was Grace Robbins, wife of best-selling author Harold Robbins. Lee and Grace were the queens of the Beverly Hills social scene, with celebrity friends all over the world, and Grace enthusiastically joined Lee in including me in every A-list party and fashion magazine and trade article. In fact, I became such a popular guest and dinner companion that *Women's Wear Daily* once referred to me as "fresh meat."

Among Grace's vast circle of friends were Saudi businessman, billionaire, and arms dealer Adnan Khashoggi and his wife Soraya. They had mansions and yachts all over the world, every one of them tended to by full-time staffs whether the Khashoggis were there or not. They also apparently had a marital "arrangement" between them that I would never have dreamed of asking about. I made that assumption one night when Grace invited Soraya, me, and Ron Ely to join her for dinner, and I got the impression that Grace thought Soraya and Ron might hit it off. They didn't. Soraya made it clear that she preferred me. She and I did get to know each other. She was a fascinating, sophisticated, generous woman who gave me a standing invitation to stay at her mews house in London whenever I was there.

Dinner parties at the home of Jules and Doris Stein. Accompanying the beautiful Polly Bergen to a gathering at Ray Stark's home. Dinner with Merle Oberon and her husband Robert Wolders one evening at Ingrid and Jerry Orbach's house. Jerry had his own wine cellar and sent back the first bottle of wine that was brought to the table.

I never took any of these invitations for granted, and sometimes I actually marveled at them. But I was a good listener, I definitely never monopolized a conversation, and apparently I was respectful since I always got invited back. And maybe, I hope, they enjoyed having me around because, regardless of "who they were," they knew I genuinely cared about them.

When I wasn't busy impressing myself with my social life, I was even busier, like so many other performers, doing my fair share of episodic television.

There are a lot of great things about guest starring on TV series episodes.

There are the paychecks, of course.

There's the wide variety of roles. I was the head of state of a South American country on *Santa Barbara*. I was a womanizing industrialist on *Wonder Woman*. I was an Italian psychic on *The Scarecrow and Mrs. King*. I was a shoplifter on *The Jackie Gleason Show*. The list goes on . . . and on . . . and on. I can honestly say I was never bored.

There's the opportunity to work with people you would never have had a chance to meet anywhere else. *Murder, She Wrote*, for example, was a show everyone wanted to do, thanks to its star, Angela Lansbury. Angela was warm and welcoming to every one of the guest stars on that show, and I somehow managed to get through filming without gushing about what a fan I'd been of hers all the way back to her MGM movie days. *The Manchurian Candidate. The Long, Hot Summer. Gaslight.* So many classic films, not to mention four Tony Awards for her Broadway musical accomplishments. She's one of the reasons you'll never hear me use the word "only" when I talk about doing episodic television.

Medical Center. Three episodes, playing an opera singer's manager, a surgeon, and a Hispanic doctor. Directed by Vincent Sherman, who back in the day directed everyone from Joan Crawford to Humphrey Bogart to Errol Flynn to Bette Davis. I loved his stories, of course, and it was such an honor to meet him and work with him; and it took a TV series to make that happen. *Dallas.* I was originally asked to do one episode, but I ended up doing eleven. It was a beautifully produced show with a great cast, and I had the most wonderful time working with the gorgeous Barbara Carrera. She and I were bad guys, teaming up together against J. R. Ewing; between takes I got to hear her stories about Peter O'Toole, and Burt Lancaster, and Sean Connery in the James Bond movie she did (*Never Say Never Again*), and even how she quit smoking with the help of an English psychic. It never ceases to amaze me when women as beautiful as Barbara turn out to be so genuinely nice.

There are the worth-waiting-for location shoots. Getting paid, for example, to take a first-class trip to Honolulu for an episode of *Hawaii Five-O*. I played a shady district attorney. The script was especially well written, and Jack Lord was a real pleasure to work with, an actor who took a lot of pride in his series and maintained a very high standard of professionalism on the set.

And then, on very rare occasions, there's the joy of finding yourself working with old friends. When I appeared on *The Carol Burnett Show*, it was the first time I'd seen Carol since we went with my friend Drusilla Davis to see the film of *West Side Story*. My fellow guest star on that episode of Carol's show was another lovely, very familiar face whom I'd work with again a few years later.

I was proud and excited to be the guest star on the final episode of *The Partridge Family*, playing the high school boyfriend of Shirley Partridge, played by my dear Shirley Jones, who shows up to renew their relationship. Our kiss goodbye was the last shot of that delightful four-season series.

Ruth Aarons was on the set every minute, of course, with four of her clients working there together—me, Shirley, David Cassidy, and Susan Dey, who played Laurie Partridge. Ruth called Shirley "Miss Wagon Train," I think because Shirley dealt so gracefully with all that happens in life, the good and sometimes not so good. And I have no idea what prompted it, but at one point while we were shooting Ruth quietly leaned over to me, indicated Shirley and David and, I guess indicating how confident they both were, said, "Why can't you be like them?" Not a bad question, actually—they were seemingly so relaxed, and I was such a worrier.

I've known very few people in my life who were more adept than Ruth Aarons at shooting herself in the foot. She had so much going

With Shirley Jones, 2010

for her in so many ways. She could be so generous, so much fun, and so fiercely loyal that she inspired loyalty from those of us who found our way into her inner circle. She could have been so much happier, and made her clients so much happier to be with her, if she hadn't buried all those good qualities under her almost pathological insistence on being a control freak.

A few years after I filmed that final *Partridge Family* episode, my agent Ina Bernstein and I went to Ruth's house one afternoon for a scheduled meeting to talk about a game plan for my career. We arrived to find her in a seething panic about Shirley Jones. Shirley's contract with Ruth had either just expired or was about to expire, and apparently Shirley was resisting re-signing with her.

I loved Shirley Jones, professionally and personally. I still do. I'm sure I'll always feel a special connection to her, since she's the one who presented me with my Academy Award. That having been said, I doubt if Ina and I would have set aside an afternoon to listen to Ruth do a two-hour monologue about Shirley and her contract; but no matter how hard we tried, we couldn't get Ruth to change the subject and talk about my career, i.e., the reason we were there in the first place.

Ruth had been unapologetically crazy about Shirley's first husband Jack Cassidy. Jack was certainly uniquely handsome. He was also very charming and very funny. Ruth and I spent many laughter-filled, lively evenings having dinner at Jack and Shirley's house when their boys were growing up. Jack and Shirley did several very big shows in Las Vegas together, and I still remember Ruth joking that Jack brought a separate suitcase just for his ties. Joan Rivers was their opening act and told them "With what this act is costing you, you must be cookin' in your room!" It's no surprise that Ruth felt very much like part of that family—Jack, Shirley, and both David and Shaun Cassidy were all clients of hers, and of her business manager's, and of her doctor's, just like me, just the way Ruth liked it.

Shirley never made a secret of the fact that Jack was the great love of her life, but they divorced in 1974. Tragically, Jack died two years later in a fire at his apartment in West Hollywood. It devastated Shirley, of course, and Ruth was almost as devastated as Shirley.

Then Shirley married actor/comedian Marty Ingels. Marty had a strong personality and a mind of his own. He had a reputation for being abrasive and combative, and he apparently saw no use for Ruth Aarons in Shirley's life. But Shirley said Marty always made her laugh. Needless to say, to put it as politely as possible, Ruth *loathed* Marty Ingels, so Shirley found herself in the terrible position of having to choose between her husband and her manager, a manager she thought so highly of that she'd asked Ruth to be the godmother to one of her sons. If Ruth had played her cards wisely, she could have found a way to get along with Marty and keep Shirley as a client, but she just couldn't bring herself to do it. She lost Shirley. And by the way, Ina and I left Ruth's house that afternoon without a word ever being said about my career.

I was in Paris in June of 1980 when I got a call from our group physician Dr. Milton Uhley, telling me that Ruth's sweet Black houseman, Lloyd, had found Ruth lying in her master bedroom shower.

There was no foul play involved. All indications were that she'd simply fallen and hit her head on the tile. Lloyd immediately called Dr. Uhley, who rushed over and, I was told later, hurriedly emptied Ruth's nightstand and the rest of the house of God knows how many bottles of pills before calling 9-1-1.

A few people who were closer to Ruth than I was, including David Cassidy, said that, unbeknownst to me, she'd become addicted to prescription medications, particularly Seconal, in her final years. I don't know that to be true, but it would help explain how erratic and irrational her behavior had become. Whatever caused it, we'd all found it impossible to ignore it or make excuses for it anymore, and by the time she passed away, Ruth had lost all of us.

I'll never know how Dr. Uhley tracked me down in Paris that day to break the news to me. I do know, though, that Ruth left her Beverly Hills house to him. None of my business, of course, but it didn't sit well with me.

I obviously still think of Ruth Aarons often. I wish she'd been the happy, successful woman we all believed she had in her somewhere. I wish I could say I always smile when I remember her, but I can't. Well, sometimes, but not always.

Chapter Fifteen

As several people close to me had predicted, my career went right on without Ruth Aarons—right on to a return in fact to the London theater. Bram Stoker's *Dracula* was enjoying a long, successful run on Broadway, with Frank Langella in the title role. He was spectacular, a bona fide leading man, imposingly tall, powerful, and charismatic, with a beautiful speaking voice and a black velvet cape lined in blood red. He was surrounded by an equally strong cast, and the Edwin Gorey sets were stunning, lots of black with small accents of red here and there. The whole production was just very special.

At the same time, *The Passion of Dracula*, starring Christopher Bernau, was succeeding off Broadway. One Dracula play was on Broadway, the other was off Broadway, so they weren't really competing with each other; and I heard from several people who'd seen both that the off-Broadway version was actually a better play. It was a dark love story, a romantic approach to the classic Dracula play, and by all accounts, the off-Broadway production was a real crowd-pleaser and enormously entertaining.

So when I was approached by Alan Cluer and Helen Montague of Backstage Productions, offering me the role of Dracula in *The Passion of Dracula* at the Queens Theatre in London, I had to think about it . . . for maybe thirty seconds. Let's see, back to the London stage . . . back to Fanny, and Pieter, and my wonderful friend Jill Bennett, and so many others I'd been missing, to do a play that sounded like fun, that was already a proven success. . . . That would be a resounding *yes*!

I was the only American in the cast. The rest were English, including some actors who were very well known in British film and theater. Our director was Clifford Williams, a Welsh theatrical director and actor, who thought it would be good if I wore a cape during rehearsals. He was right. It helped me get in character . . . a little.

Once rehearsals were underway, it became apparent that a few of the actors had particular styles that were familiar to and appreciated by their British audiences, and they'd decided to maintain those signature styles in *The Passion of Dracula* to please their fans. As a general rule, that can work. In certain situations, though, it's not necessarily appropriate.

My first line of dialogue in the play was, predictably, Dracula's iconic, "Good evening." In the early stages of rehearsals I was getting more and more nervous when the time came for my entrance and that opening line—those actors, true to the personas that had made them so popular, kept responding to their first sight of Count Dracula with something bordering on nonchalance, as if I were their next door neighbor stopping by for tea.

I was having a hard enough time convincing *me* that I was Count Dracula. It didn't help to be greeted onstage by a cast who, with every good intention, didn't really seem to be buying it either. I couldn't be Dracula by myself. I needed the other actors to react with uneasiness, some awareness that something dark and dangerous had entered the room, something they're instinctively frightened of without really knowing why.

It's been said many times that Ingrid Bergman and many other leading ladies helped Cary Grant be Cary Grant because of the way they reacted to him. I'm not for a second comparing myself to Cary Grant, I'm just making a point of how important the reaction of the other actors in a scene can be. Cary Grant brought plenty of his own charm and charisma to every role he played, but his co-stars' responses to him helped confirm to the audience that those qualities were real and powerful and had an impact.

But rehearsals went on with Mr. Williams not saying much, either to me or to the other actors, and me perpetually braced for my "Good evening" to be replied to with, "Oh, hi, George. What's with the cape?" Finally I mustered up the courage to sit down with him and discuss my problem. He listened and he understood, and he had a talk about it with the cast. They understood too, and adjusted their reactions to my entrance. Thanks to that simple adjustment, I started to "feel" Dracula. I think the fact that I was able to express myself to the director and not be dismissed by him and my castmates was a real turning point for me in my performance. I started to believe in myself and in what I was doing as an actor, and let's face it, if I didn't believe it, why should anyone else? I ended up making some choices in that role that felt good and very brave, and once I got out of my own way and "went for it," I was off to the races.

We had a fantastic set for *The Passion of Dracula*, with lots of dry ice for the heavy mist that created a perfect mood and cleverly devised trap doors so that Dracula could magically appear and disappear in the blink of an eye. The costumes, the effects, the production, everything was done beautifully. It felt right because it *was* right, and the audiences had a great time taking the ride. We opened to positive reviews, and I was happy about that! I even had the privilege of being given a dressing room that had previously been occupied by Maggie Smith.

Two of my fellow actors in particular—Roy Dotrice as Professor Van Helsing and Geraldine James as Dr. Helga Van Zandt, both part of the team trying to save poor Mina from Dracula's evil clutches—were wonderful. Geraldine went out of her way to be supportive, both onstage and off. She's gone on to do some extraordinary work in such prestigious pieces as *The Jewel in the Crown*, *Gandhi*, and the film of *Downton Abbey*.

Brava, Geraldine, and thank you again.

And then, as if one vampire in London's West End wasn't enough, along came the *other* Dracula: the Frank Langella/Broadway *Dracula*, with Terence Stamp in the title role. I'd met Terence many years earlier when he was dating one of the girls in *West Side Story*, and he'd since become a huge star, with more than fifty films to his credit and a well-deserved Oscar nomination for *Billy Budd*. *Dracula* was opening at the Shaftesbury Theatre right up the road from us, which meant not just competition but potentially tough competition, and all any of us could do about it was hope for the best for everyone. I even designed and sent a Dracula-themed card to Terence on his opening night, sincerely wishing him and the *Dracula* company a long, successful run.

But for reasons no one ever quite understood, despite Terence Stamp and a really terrific production, *Dracula* didn't work and closed after two weeks.

Lydia and Charlton Heston visit me backstage after a performance on *The Passion of Dracula*, 1978.

One of many pleasant surprises during *The Passion of Dracula* was the night that Charlton Heston and his wife Lydia came to see the play. I hadn't seen him since we filmed *Diamond Head* together many years earlier. He and I weren't always on the same page politically, but other than that I couldn't have enjoyed and respected him more. He was a very nice man and I really liked him. I went into *Diamond Head* as aware as the rest of the world of his powerful onscreen presence. It was wonderful to see how seriously he took his craft—rather than just falling back on being Charlton Heston, as he could have done with no complaints from anyone, he actually went to dailies with a legal pad and took notes on his performance. It was also fun to discover that he had an unapologetic competitive streak in him, which came out during regular poker games in his dressing room between him, me, and our co-star James Darren. (I met Jimmy for the first time on that movie, by the way, and he and his wife Evy and I are still good friends to this day.)

All of us involved in *The Passion of Dracula* had a wonderful time during our almost- one-year run. It was an experience I wouldn't have missed for anything.

I was still enjoying London, and working with Nana Mouskouri at the BBC, when my New York agent Eric Shepherd called with an offer I certainly hadn't seen coming: a play called *Hokucho-Ki*, to be produced in Tokyo. What?

I have to admit, I was curious. On one hand, I barely spoke a word of Japanese. I couldn't imagine how I would even know when it was my turn to speak onstage, let alone deliver a performance that would amount to anything more than a phonetic recitation.

On the other hand, I'd been in love with Japan and its people from the moment I first landed in Tokyo to film *Flight from Ashiya*. The kindness, the courtesy, the respect, so many qualities I'd been raised with, fit my sensibilities. Like London, it was a place I'd never been before that immediately felt like home. I'd been back to Japan many times since then, working with some companies there and singing and dancing at personal appearances, and I was always deeply moved by how graciously I was welcomed on every single trip.

Fortunately, I had the perfect person to turn to for advice about whether or not I should accept this offer to tackle a play in Japan. Over the years I'd become very good friends with an amazing woman named Kazuko Komori, a well-known Japanese film critic, journalist, and highly respected member of the international press. Komori-san was a beautiful, sensitive soul who'd been a close friend of James Dean and visited his grave every year. She invited me to visit her at her hotel whenever she was in L.A., and she always insisted I bring my darling Italian Greyhound Sami so that she could spend time with both of us. She loved Sami.

With my darling Italian greyhound, Sami, 1990

My great friend Kuzuko Komori, 1985

I told Komori-san about the theater offer and asked her advice, and she immediately started looking into it. "Hakucho-Ki," the title of the play, translated to "White Butterfly Diary," she said, and the play itself was based on the tragic Madame Butterfly story. The theater where it was being produced was one of Tokyo's most prestigious venues, the Takarazuka Theater. It was being cast with major Japanese stars, and the director, Fukuko Ishii, was a star in her own right.

She encouraged me to say yes. I did, and it was a pure joy from beginning to end.

Hakucho-Ki turned out to be intelligently written. My character spoke both Japanese and English, and my dialogue was kept to a minimum without disrupting the momentum of the storytelling. Rehearsals were a continuous, fascinating challenge. As I was working on my Japanese dialogue, I devised a method that allowed me to know what I was saying and not just focus on pronouncing things properly, and of course to actually know what the other actors were saying as well. It was interesting to me that even in the early stages of rehearsing, when I was still struggling to understand the other actors' lines, I could easily recognize and appreciate what extraordinary performers they were.

The lead actress was a very famous Japanese film and theater star named Yoshiko Sakuma. Fukuko Ishii, our director, is still producing and directing today, at the age of ninety-four. I was in Japan last year for a *West Side Story* event and went to visit her at the TBS studios, where she was in the midst of yet another project she was directing. Ishii-san created the most stunning, almost balletic entrance for Miss Sakuma. Wearing a traditional but elaborate kimono and traditional black wig, she entered down a ramp, very slowly, every sensuous movement filled with drama and breathtaking physicality, all accompanied by the live orchestra in the pit. It was hypnotic. I've never seen an entrance, before or since, that compared to it.

From time to time, single voices in the audience would discreetly say her name, "Sakuma," which I learned is considered a huge compliment in the Japanese theater world. Once while I was onstage I heard someone quietly say "Chakiris," and I was thrilled.

It was truly an honor to work with such spectacular artists, and it was Miss Ishii and Kazuko Komori who made it happen. I've never been to Japan since then without making sure that Miss Ishii is the first person I see.

That unforgettable time in Tokyo also introduced me to a very touching tradition that I wish more theaters would embrace.

Upon arriving at the Takarazuka Theater every day before a performance, it was important to stop and kneel before a shrine that was a permanent fixture in the theater, to pay respect to the experience we were all about to share together. It was a silent, deeply personal reminder to appreciate the uniqueness of what can happen for those onstage and for those in the audience, and an acknowledgement of the connection between the two that is the essence of the theatrical tradition.

Who knows, maybe it was my daily visits to that shrine that paved the way for my life to intersect with one of the most profound theatrical opportunities of my career—the English tour of a magnificent play by David Henry Hwang called, coincidentally or not, *M. Butterfly*.

M. Butterfly is the story of Rene Gallimard, a French diplomat posted in Peking who falls in love with Song Liling, a Chinese opera star. Song becomes Gallimard's mistress and, over the course of their twenty-year relationship, manages to keep him from discovering that not only is she a spy for the Communist Chinese, she also happens to be a man. In the end, Gallimard, horrified and devastatingly betrayed, commits suicide while Song dispassionately watches.

I played Rene Gallimard in the English tour, a role originated on Broadway by John Lithgow and later played by Clive Owen in the Broadway revival. *M. Butterfly* is the kind of material that makes the theater a gold mine for actors in search of meaningful roles, made even more powerful by the fact that David Henry Hwang's play is based on a true story. It was an invaluable bonus for me and my performance that he came to spend a few days with us.

Our producer was Bill Kenwright, one of the most prolific producers in British theater, credited with almost every play in the West End at the time. Our director was Richard Olivier.

We couldn't have asked for a more superb director than Richard Olivier. He was quiet and centered, with a lovely sense of humor; and despite being the son of Sir Laurence Olivier, he never let his ego get in the way. No night at the theater was ever "his." It was always ours, and the audience's. He understood the complexities of the play. And maybe most of all, he had a clear perspective on how each of his actors arrived at their individual performances. Like every other theatrical director, he gave notes after every rehearsal and performance. But he allowed each of us to move forward in our own way without censoring ourselves, maybe even surprise ourselves with some unexpected discoveries, and then discuss afterwards what was worth keeping and what wasn't. The kind of freedom Richard Olivier encouraged builds confidence, and it's an exciting, exhilarating way to work.

We were also blessed with costume and set designers who brilliantly overcame a real challenge. The original *M. Butterfly* production featured spectacular, opulent Oriental costumes and sets. Since our sets and wardrobe would have to travel, our designers kept it simple but still beautiful, creating a multilevel set, Oriental in style, with different playing areas. I actually thought it served the play even better than the original—the simplicity kept the focus on the actors and the play itself, without the distraction of elaborate sets and costumes. *M. Butterfly* is about so much more than that.

As for our cast, we were a great company of professionals, with a brilliant young Asian actor named Darren Chan playing opera star Song Liling. The final scene required him to be nude, which was an interesting challenge/dynamic for him, the other actors, and ultimately the audience, of course. In the early stages of rehearsal Darren remained clothed—no one expected him to strip naked every day in a cold rehearsal room. But inevitably the day arrived when it happened, not just for Darren but for all of us, that moment of "Oh, my God, he's nude!" It took a little time for everyone to adjust. It wasn't gratuitous nudity, though; it was essential to the story, and because we understood that and believed passionately in what we were doing, we quickly got over it for the sake of the play. After all, "the show must go on."

We had such a magnificent time together, and we were enthusiastically received by our audiences and the critics as well. I'd learned over the years to never read reviews until the run is over—at least for me, they get in the way. I don't need to be distracted by what anyone but the director thinks of what I'm doing while I'm working. Cast members who did read the reviews told me that they were unanimous raves. That was nice to hear, obviously, and I have to say, it didn't surprise me. I could feel it. And thanks to an incredible cast and crew, and to David Henry Hwang and Bill Kenwright and Richard Olivier, it was that strong a production, and that special a night in the theater.

I was so moved by the whole experience that when I arrived back home after the tour, I took out a full page ad in *Variety* with a photo of me in the role and some of those rave reviews. Very unlike me, but I couldn't help it: I was so proud.

Chapter Sixteen

More films, more TV, more theatrical productions . . . some better than others, but not one of them taken for granted or unappreciated.

I'm sitting here looking back on my life and feeling so blessed.

I was given an extraordinary family who've always made me feel loved and valued and never, ever alone.

I was given extraordinary friends who've done exactly the same and still do.

And I was born with an extraordinary passion that at times opened every door that might have stayed closed without it, a passion for dancing.

Like every other dancer I know, dancing isn't just part of what we do, it's part of who we are.

Since I first became a student at the American School of Dance when I was nineteen years old, I never let a day go by without a dance class. No day was complete without it. I always bundled up in an overcoat on my way to class, in the winter and in the summer. I didn't want to wait until I was physically warm from the exercise. I wanted to start being warm when I left the house and stay warm through the entire class, and then finish the class with stretching.

There was no such thing as a day off, no matter where I was—London, Paris, Rome, Spain, Tokyo, anywhere and everywhere, I took a class. One very cold, snowy winter day in London, I went back to the dressing room after class to discover that my shoes were gone. I walked home through deep snow in my socks. I don't recommend it, but taking that class was worth it.

Whether the other dancers in class and I could understand each other verbally or not, we understood each other perfectly when class began and the dancing started. We were all fluent in the universal language of music and movement. Any other possible barriers between us disappeared, and we were suddenly a studio of like-minded people with the same objectives—to somehow keep improving, to try to be better than we were the day before, to keep getting stronger and more supple, to stretch beyond what would ever be esthetically correct, to achieve that "line," that shape, knowing that "going beyond" made it more possible to get it right.

Dancers almost always have a great sense of humor. We take our training very seriously, but never ourselves. We dig deep and expose every fiber of our being while dancing, which is humanizing, humbling, and exquisitely unifying. And like every other athletic endeavor, the bar is constantly being raised, and each new generation of dancers has to meet those new challenges and more. There's no such thing as resting on your laurels, or stopping at "good enough."

Dancing, when it's your passion, demands everything you've got to give it, which I happily gave. In return, it gave me a lifetime of being part of that magic I dreamed of when I was a boy sneaking off to the movies, and especially, part of the most amazing magic of all, the magic called *West Side Story* that continues to define the phrase "the gift that keeps on giving."

Countless screenings, interviews, and events all over the world that continue to this day. Countless trips to sit in audiences as an honored guest and watch local productions . . . discovering that no matter how far away the country or how small the town where those local productions were appearing, every member of every cast feels like family.

The fortieth anniversary of *West Side Story* was celebrated with a screening of the film on October 6, 2001, at Radio City Music Hall. At the request of our host, Turner Classic Movies, I had a beautiful poster signed by everyone involved, which led me to a long-overdue introduction—for the first time, when I went to his house to get his signature, I met Ernest Lehman, the man who wrote the *West Side Story* screenplay, based on the book by Arthur Laurents. I never understood why Arthur Laurents didn't write the screenplay, or how he felt about Ernest Lehman writing it instead. But it was a pleasure to meet Mr. Lehman, who was warm and lovely and appreciated being asked to sign that poster. He told

West Side Story cast reunion at the Hollywood Bowl, 1994

Walter Mirisch, Rita Moreno, Russ
Tamblyn, and me behind Robert
Wise, 1995

me he'd gone to Paris for a *West Side Story* celebration and discovered that the lobby card didn't have his name on it, so he wrote it there himself. As he should have.

The fiftieth anniversary . . . November 5, 2011 . . . a red-carpet Blu-ray premiere of *West Side Story* at Grauman's Chinese Theatre . . . Rita, Russ, and I leaving our footprints and signatures in the cement of that historic forecourt . . . remembering those quiet nights, walking past Grauman's on my way back to my boardinghouse room after finishing my custodial duties at the American School of Dance and always stopping to imagine the constellation of brilliant stars who had stood right there once and literally left their footprints for the rest of us to follow.

And now, here I am, almost ten years later, seeing *West Side Story*, the indelible experience that started so much of my life, come full circle, with a whole new life of its own. It fills me with the greatest renewed sense of gratitude and pride.

Grauman's Chinese Theater hand and foot ceremony with Rita Moreno and Russ Tamblyn, 2011

I'm forever grateful to the great achievements of Jerome Robbins, Leonard Bernstein, Arthur Laurents, and Stephen Sondheim. They started it. They made it happen. They brought it to the theater, and to the screen . . . thousands of theaters and thousands of screens . . . and the beat goes on. They touched the hearts and imaginations of countless people with a creation that speaks to basic human truths and feelings, socially and politically.

Thanks to those four men, I've had the honor of being part of that legacy, and that is an amazing gift.

We each have so many stories in our lives. It's incredible that my stories include one with so much value, that continues to give not only to me but to all who've been a part of it in productions over the years, and to audiences around the world.

There have been nonstop productions of *West Side Story* since its premiere on Broadway in 1957, and there will be many more, along with the already opened but COVID-interrupted 2020 Broadway production and the upcoming Steven Spielberg film. How many achievements in theater and film can say that?

I think the answer is: one. *West Side Story*, a dazzling, irreplaceable work. It inspires audiences, and it inspires everyone who takes part in keeping its unprecedented legacy alive.

That is why I will always cherish, respect, and owe more than I can ever repay to "My West Side Story."

Thank you for a wonderful life!

Film, Theater, and Television Credits and Awards and Appearances

1947—*Song of Love* (Film)
1951—*The Great Caruso* (Film)
1952—*Stars and Stripes Forever* (Film)
1953—*Gentlemen Prefer Blondes* (Film)
1953—*Give a Girl a Break* (Film)
1953—*Second Chance* (Film)
1953—*The President's Lady* (Film)
1953—*The 5,000 Fingers of Dr. T.* (Film)
1954—*Brigadoon* (Film)
1954—*The Country Girl* (Film
1954—*There's No Business Like Show Business* (Film)
1954—*White Christmas* (Film)
1955—*The Girl Rush* (Film)
1956—*Meet Me in Las Vegas* (Film)
1957—*Under Fire* (Film)
1958—*West Side Story* (Theater) Her Majesty's Theater London
1961—*West Side Story* (Film)
1962—Academy Award, Best Actor in a Supporting Role
1962—*Diamond Head* (Film)
1962—Golden Globe Award, Best Actor in a Supporting Role
1962—*Two and Two Make Six* (Film)
1963—*Kings of the Sun* (Film)
1963—*The Ed Sullivan Show* (TV Series)
1964—*633 Squadron* (Film)
1964—*Bebo's Girl* (Film)
1964—*Flight from Ashiya* (Film)
1964–1967—Capitol Record Recordings (4 albums)
1965—*McGuire, Go Home!* (Film)
1966—*Is Paris Burning?* (Film)

1966—*The Theft of the Mona Lisa* (Film)
1967—*Kismet* (TV Movie)
1967—Personal Appearance, Caesar's Palace, Las Vegas
1967—*The Andy Williams Show* (TV Series)
1967—*The Young Girls of Rochefort* (Film)
1968—*One Life to Live* (TV Series)
1968—*The Carol Burnet Show* (TV Series)
1968—*The Day the Hot Line Got Hotter* (Film)
1969—Personal Appearance (Riviera Hotel, Las Vegas)
1969—Personal Appearance (Mexico & Australia)
1969—*Sharon in Red* (Film, Spain)
1969—*The Big Cube* (Film)
1969—*The Corn is Green* (Theater) (Ivanhoe Theater, Chicago)
1969—*The Jackie Gleason Show* (TV Series)
1970—Personal Appearance (Harrah's Hotel, Reno)
1970–1975—*Medical Center* (TV Series)
1971—*Company* (Theater) (National Tour)
1972—*Hawaii Five-O* (TV Series)
1973—*Police Surgeon* (TV Series)
1974—*Guys and Dolls* (Theater) (Millwaukee)
1974—*Notorious Woman* (TV Mini-Series)
1974—*The Partridge Family* (TV Series)
1974—*Thriller* (TV Series)
1975—*Nana Mouskouri French TV Special*
1975—Personal Appearance Show (Salle Pleyel, Paris)
1975—Personal Appearance Show (Sporting Club, Monte Carlo)
1975—*Ten from the Twenties* (British ITV Series)
1976—*George Chakiris French TV Special "Numero Un"*
1978—*Dracula* (Theater) (Queen's Theater, London)
1978—*Why Not Stay for Breakfast?* (Film)
1978—*Wonder Woman* (TV Series)
1978–1982—*Fantasy Island* (TV Series)
1979—*Elizabeth the Queen* (Theater) (Buffalo Arena Theater, New York)
1979—*Hakucho Ki "White Butterfly Diary"* (Theater) (Takarazuka Theater, Tokyo)

1979—*The Fantasticks* (Theater) (Dallas)
1980—*Camelot* (Theater) (Little Theater on the Square, Illinois)
1981—*Hakucho Ki "White Butterfly Diary"* (Film for Japanese Television)
1981—*My Fair Lady* (Theater) (Little Theater on the Square, Illinois)
1982—*I Do, I Do* (Theater) (Dallas)
1983—*CHiPs* (TV Series)
1983–1984—*Matt Houston* (TV Series)
1984—*Nihon No Omokage "Glimpses of Unfamiliar Japan"* (NHK Japanese TV Mini-Series)
1984—Personal Appearance Tour, Japan
1984—*Poor Little Rich Girls* (British ITV Series)
1984—*Scarecrow and Mrs. King* (TV Series)
1985—*Hell Town* (TV Series)
1985–1986—*Dallas* (TV Series)
1986—Personal Appearance Tour, Japan
1988—*Santa Barbara* (TV Series)
1989—*Murder, She Wrote* (TV Series) Eric Bowman (Guest Star)
1989—*Stop the World I Want to Get Off* (Theater) (Burt Reynolds Theater, Florida)
1989—*The Music Man* (Theater)
1989–1990—*Superboy* (TV Series)
1990—*Pale Blood* (Film)
1992—*Human Target* (TV Series)
1992—*M. Butterfly* (Theater) (English National Tour)
1994—*Jane Eyre* (Theater) (English National Tour)
1995—*Les Filles du Lido* (French TV Mini-Series)
1996—*Last of the Summer Wine* (British TV Series)
2015—*In Your Arms* (Theater) (Old Globe Theater, San Diego)
2020—*Not To Forget* (Post-production) (Film)

Index